SOUTH YORKSHIRE WALKS:
30 Classic Routes

Martin Smith

Published by Sigma Leisure – an imprint of
Sigma Press, 1 South Oak Lane, Wilmslow, Cheshire SK9 6AR, England.

British Library Cataloguing in Publication Data
A CIP record for this book is available from the British Library.

ISBN: 1-85058-411-7

Typesetting and Design by: Sigma Press, Wilmslow, Cheshire.

Cover photographs: On Wharncliffe Crags *(Martin Smith)*; Conisbrough Castle *(Duncan Smith)*

Maps and photographs: the author

Printed by: MFP Design & Print

Disclaimer: the information in this book is given in good faith and is believed to be correct at the time of publication. No responsibility is accepted by either the author or publisher for errors or omissions, or for any loss or injury howsoever caused. Only you can judge your own fitness, competence and experience.

CONTENTS

Introduction

The Walks

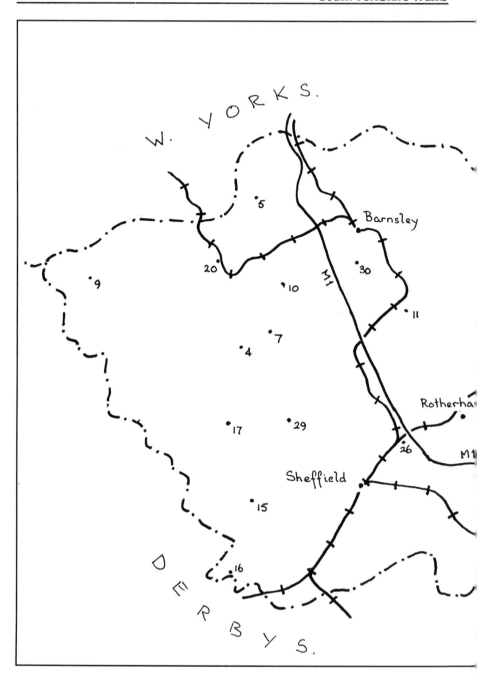

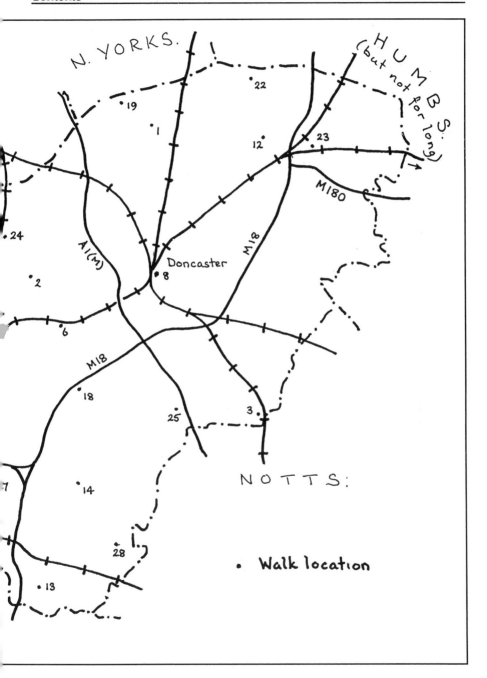

KEY TO MAPS:

Road used for walk

Track used for walk

Obvious footpath used for walk

Intermittent footpath used for walk

No obvious path, but route of walk

Other road

Other track

Other obvious footpath

Other intermittent footpath

Railway

River, arrow shows direction of flow

Church/Chapel

South Yorkshire: A County of Hidden Delights

This book covers the whole of South Yorkshire. Walks elsewhere in the Peak District and South Pennines can be found in several other books published by Sigma Leisure.

To many people, the very name South Yorkshire will conjure up a picture of coal mines and pit heaps, steel works and slag. It is true that the economic base of the county is, or was, in these basic, heavy industries, but to dismiss South Yorkshire as a walking area because of its industry is to do the area a great disservice. The county comprises the four big urban areas of Barnsley, Doncaster, Rotherham and Sheffield. Two of these pride themselves as containing a piece of Britain's Premier National Park, the Peak District, whilst Doncaster dabbles its toes in the tidal waters of the river from which it takes its name. In between the high wild moors of the west and the low-lying peatlands of the east, is a county of great diversity, including gritstone cliffs, delightful wooded valleys, limestone scenery and a wealth of industrial archeology. The coalfield belt stretches throughout the central part of the county, but don't let that put you off. The industry that shows up graphically on the old One Inch to the Mile maps, is rapidly vanishing, taking thousands of jobs with it and changing whole communities. However, the disfigurement that the mines and their attendant heavy industries wrought is being reinstated by the various local authorities, with a large measure of assistance from Nature. Where once there was soot and grime there are now fields, wild flowers and delightful walks.

South Yorkshire has no County Council, being merely a "geographical expression", so maintenance and signing of paths is largely the responsibility of the individual metropolitan boroughs, Barnsley, Doncaster, Rotherham and the City of Sheffield, though some Parish and Town councils have arrangements to maintain paths in their areas. Similarly some voluntary groups have adopted paths to keep them open and in good repair. Any problems should first be addressed to the Borough or City Councils. You should have no difficulty in finding the paths, all the boroughs take their footpath responsibilities very seriously.

Towpaths along the British Waterways canals are not always rights of way. They are usually permissive paths, but can be closed at will by British Waterways, particularly where canal maintenance is in progress. This should be respected. Similarly there are other permissive paths mentioned in this book, of which the most important are those along Wharncliffe Crags. These are sufficiently well used and popular to be waymarked in places, but that doesn't alter their status. Again they can be closed at will, so be prepared.

There is a great contrast in the users of the paths in this county. The paths on the western fringe of the county, forming part of the Peak District, see regular use by the rucksack-toting hiker. Sheffield must be one of the few cities where you can walk down the main shopping street in hiking breeches and boots and not look a complete freak. The paths in the central part of the county are used more by locals, dog walking or strolling, or even going to work or shopping. Designer boots, breeches and waterproofs look singularly out of place here. Even a rucksack is greeted with a raised eyebrow. The eastern, rural paths see little local use, so the only walkers you are likely to see are discerning people like yourself, refugees from the National Park "motorways". Again, designer gear is likely to be the source of a wry smile, but carry a well-thumbed OS Pathfinder Map and wear a pair of well-worn boots and this will quickly lead to a chat about the conflicts between farmers and walkers, or other staples like the weather, beer and the ruination of footpaths because of "too many guide books". At this point, hide your book and suddenly remember an urgent appointment!

Public Transport

Rural bus and train travel is an interesting experience in its own right and can be as much fun as the walk or the session in the local pub. All the walks in this book can be accessed by public transport. South Yorkshire Passenger Transport Executive (SYPTE) is the agency responsible for public transport publicity and signing of the bus stops, and a good job they make of it too. Even in the most deeply-rural areas there is the ubiquitous SYPTE bus stop and timetable case. If you are using the bus or train you should always check times in advance, especially since the deregulation of bus services introduced a plethora of operators. SYPTE no longer attempt to produce a comprehensive timetable or system map because of the frequency of changes. They do however produce individual service leaflets, which are obtainable from the main enquiry offices in the towns.

The PTE also runs a telephone inquiry service for would be travellers: 01709 515151. Rail information is also available from this number, but ring British Rail for more detailed information about times and fares. Their number is 0114 272 6411. In future the rail services in this area will be franchised out to private operators, but SYPTE will be able to keep a watching brief on them and provide the required details.

The Walks

There are 30 walks for you to choose from, varying from 3 to 11 miles. Obviously the exertion required varies too. There are steep ascents and miles of bog covered moor on the fringes of the Peak District, but, for the most part, South Yorkshire is a tamed and gentle country for walkers, though deeply rural and lonely in parts. However, as mentioned in other books in this series, there are a few golden rules to follow.

Whilst you don't need designer gear for these walks, a stout pair of boots or walking shoes are essential. Even strolling along the Sheffield Canal towpath, it is best to go prepared with a light rucksack, waterproofs, a spare jumper and a snack. Most other people you meet will be out fishing or going for an afternoon stroll a few hundred yards from their front door. Arguably they don't need such equipment, but you do. There's nothing worse than travelling home in wet clothes. You can always do what the author and his wife did. Carry a small rucksack on the walk and include in it a less conspicuous carrier bag in which the rucksack goes for the tram journey. The weather can be notoriously fickle, even in central Sheffield. Beware the comment from the passing local that, "There'll be some watter goin' o'er t'weir t'night!" Head for the shelter of the nearest hostelry and sit out the approaching deluge.

It's always a good idea to let someone know where you are going. This is not to say that you should display a notice on your car. That would be asking for trouble, but a word with your neighbour or a friend would be no bad thing. Even though you're not going mountaineering, some of these walks are on paths that see very little use and are surprisingly remote. An accident here and you'd not be found for days.

Maps

The walks should be easy to follow using the instructions and maps in the book. However, for each walk the appropriate OS Pathfinder map (1:25000 scale), is indicated. These maps show every field boundary, right of way, track and stream. They also show a wealth of additional detail, which cannot be included in a book of this nature. I strongly recommend that you invest in some of these maps, though I do acknowledge that to buy the number required to cover all the walks is rather a daunting prospect, unless you are intending to do some exploration of your own in the same area. Many public libraries have a map lending service, so this possibility should be examined. Alternatively the OS 1:50000 sheets cover a much larger area and whilst they lack the fine detail, they do at least show the paths. Don't just rely on the maps in the book. With the best will in the world, you could take a wrong turning and be completely lost without a wider ranging map. The more urban walks do not show up well on either the 1:25000 or 1:50000 series. For these a larger scale still is really required, but this book should give sufficiently adequate description to enable you to avoid falling into the canal or ending up in some steel stockholder's yard.

Respect the countryside

You must remember that the countryside and the towns are not just a playground for you. Both are working environments. Respect it, respect those who work in it and those who live in it. Make sure you leave it no worse for your visit, even if some other visitors are obviously less scrupulous.

1. Askern

The Route: Askern, Askern Common, Alder Wood, Heyworth Lane, Copley Spring Wood, East Coast Main Line, Moss, Star Farm, Brick Kiln Lane, Back Lane, Barcroft Gates (ECML), Haywood, Long Bank, Rushy Moor Plantation, Askern.

Distance: 9km (5½ miles)

Start: Askern Pond car park. GR. 563136

Map(s): OS 1:25000 Pathfinder Series No. 704 Hemsworth and Askern

How to get there:

By public transport: There is a frequent daily bus service from Doncaster to Askern. There's a railway too, but unfortunately no station.

By car: from south or north follow the A19 into the centre of Askern and then follow the sign to Sykehouse and Fishlake. In about 100 metres from the A19 there is a car park entrance on the right.

The Walk

A lakeside path

Make your way from the car park, past the buildings that make up the Health Centre complex, and so reach the lakeside. There is a cafe here and boating in season, but of course you are not interested in such things. Turn left and walk along the lakeside path, away from the cafe. At the southern end of the lake the path goes right, but you should carry on across the grass, with the ditch and the woodyard to your right. You rapidly leave the manicured green of the lakeside park behind and come into a rough grassed area.

Spires and cooling towers

The more obvious path continues ahead, over a footbridge across the stream. However, this is not your route. Instead, turn left just before the bridge and follow a hazy path along the north bank until you come up against the railway line. A stile takes you onto the railway, which you cross on the level, despite the map indicating a footbridge. Take great care here, especially if you have children with you. This crossing is a useful foretaste of what is to come later. Another stile takes you back into fields again. The playing fields and houses of Askern Common are to the left, whilst to the right is the ditch. Follow the well-blazed track straight ahead, ignoring all turns to left or right. The spire of Haywood church can be seen to the right across the fields. So too can the towers of Thorpe Marsh power station.

Tunnel of trees

About a kilometre away from the railway crossing you go over a sleeper bridge and continue ahead with the hedge and ditch to your right. The path bears left at the end of the field, to reach a stile in the far corner. Turn right just beyond the stile and follow the ditch and hedge until you reach Alder Wood. The path passes through the wood in a veritable tunnel of trees of many varieties, including oak, birch and sycamore. Beyond the wood, follow the inevitable ditch until you reach a junction of paths and tracks. These all boast their own signs. You should turn left at this point, following the bridleway sign. This track soon leads to Heyworth Lane, which is a real road. The map indicates that you are at the dizzy height of 6 metres above sea level at this point. Turn right, along the road.

Leaden boots

After about 150 metres of road walking, there is a sign post on the left, just before Copley Spring Wood. The name indicates that the wood was once managed as a coppice. Leave the road here and go through the gap into the field. The temptation is to stick close to the right hand side of the field, alongside the wood. However, the path bears away from the wood, crossing the field diagonally to reach a signpost, whose whereabouts is indicated by some poplars. Navigation has not been helped by the removal of the left hand boundary of the field. The passage of this field was accompanied by the growing worry that some kind soul had put quantities of lead in the author's boots. Closer inspection revealed nothing worse than a three inch layer of mud. At the signpost, pass through a gap in the hedge near the concrete block. Which insane character saw fit to put a lump of concrete in such an out of the way spot?

In the next field, continue alongside the left hand hedge, noting to the right the low embankment which carries the electrified East Coast Main Line. Noting too the speed at which the trains pass! Between 160 and 200 km/hr. Calculate how long you have got to cross the line if you see a train coming.

Across the London to Edinburgh railway

The map shows a pond on the left, but this is well-hidden by trees and hedges, until you are almost past it. At the end of the field, a gap in the hedge takes you into a small area of scrub, from which a stile leads up to the railway. Cross with great care and as quickly as possible. Note that there are no planks between the rails, so you will be walking on ballast and sleepers. On the other side another stile takes you back into fields again. There is the inevitable ditch on the left. Continue straight ahead, through two fields, the first being exited by a gap in the hedge, the second by a stile. In the third field, the map indicates a junction of paths. This is not obvious on the ground. Indeed, a hunt for the "straight on" route failed to find a way out of the field. Fortunately, the way this walk goes does not rely on the "straight on" route, but turns left and crosses a bridge to a stile in the hedge. Beyond the stile is the children's playground of the The Star pub, just a stone's throw from the East Coast Main Line and perfect for train spotters.

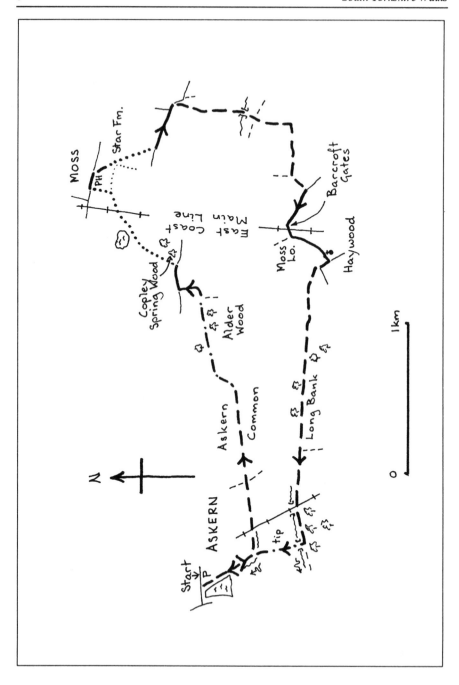

The Star

Star Farm

From the pub, turn right and walk along Moss Road for about 70 metres. Then turn right, along the track leading to Star Farm. As you near the farm, you will look in vain for any sign to indicate where the path goes. A query to the farmer elicited the response that few people used the path so no-one bothered to sign it. However, there was no problem about using the route. The farmer also volunteered the information that Star Farm had once been the pub and the path we were seeking had then been the road. Skirt to the left of the farm buildings, with the field on your left. At the end of the buildings the field broadens out and there is a waymark on the right. This is also the point at which the "straight on" route, mentioned in the previous paragraph, should join. Needless to say, there is no sign of it, so it is just as well you decided to visit the pub. At this point the path across the field forks. The map shows a field boundary just to the left, but this has gone. Close scrutiny of the far boundary, straight ahead, will reveal two footpath signs, one to the left, the other to the right. You want the one to the left. Make a bee-line across the field to the stile and thus gain Heyworth Lane again. Here go left. After about 400 metres there is a junction of lanes and tracks. This is Brick Kiln Lane and here you go right, following the bridleway signs.

Hippopotamus country!

The bridleway is bordered by ditches and hedges. The reconnaissance notes simply say, "Mud". Follow the bridleway until a gate is reached. The waymarked route doesn't pass through the gate, but goes right and then left over the bridge. This seems singularly pointless as both the gate and bridge lead into the same field, but who are we to argue. In the next field the bridleway bears diagonally right. You can't miss the path. It is well-defined as a swathe of mud. At the far side of the field there is a junction of tracks, which are waymarked. Your route is still the bridleway, which goes roughly straight on, over the bridge. You are now heading towards the old windmill which can be seen ahead at Wrancarr Mill. However, before you reach the mill there is another junction of tracks, just after another bridge. Turn right at the junction, along Back Lane. At this point, it is gratifying to note that you can now see the water tower at Askern. At least you are going in the right direction, but it seems a long way off.

Barcroft Gates

A T-junction is soon reached and here you should turn left, still following Back Lane. A further 150 metres brings you to Wrancarr Lane, where you turn right. Haywood church spire is visible to the left, with the looming shapes of the cooling towers of Eggborough and Drax power stations to the right. A quick trot along Wrancarr Lane leads to Barcroft Gates. This period piece level crossing over the East Coast Main Line, is still manned. The crossing keeper cheerfully asked us to wait as a train was due. When asked what was the alternative, he made some reference to strawberry jam, but the rest of his reasoning was drowned as a train thundered through. The advice to all walkers is to heed the keeper's warning.

Once you are safely across the lines, carry on along the lane, passing the craft centre on the right. Soon Haywood church is reached. Disappointingly this turns out to be disused and semi derelict, but one has to ask what population it would serve in any case, for there is no village here. Just beyond the church, turn right at the road junction. Where this lane swings to the left, just beyond the bungalow, there is a track on the right. This is your route. Almost at once after leaving the road, the track swings left alongside a hedge. There is neither stile nor gate at the end of this field, just a gap in a hedge which takes you through to another field. Now the hedge is on your left. Soon the track bears off to the right. This is not shown on the OS map.

Along Long Bank

The path continues alongside the hedge and ditch to a waymarked stile. Straight on here, with a ditch, fence and hedge on your left. The path soon reaches a small wood on the left and then a waymarked stile. Continue ahead, still with the ditch and hedge to the left. A glance at the map will show that this section is known as Long Bank. This is an apt name, for the boundary on the left consists of a ditch, hedge and an earth bank. Sometimes the path occupies the top of the bank, other times it runs at the foot. The field to the right is rough and "unimproved", with some scrubby bushes. Soon you will spot a stile on the left, but this should be ignored. Continue ahead along the bank, which is now covered with trees. However, they don't look too healthy and there is little or no sign of any new growth or saplings. At the end of this wooded section, a single plank bridge spans a stream. The plank is slippery so take care. Beyond the bridge a ladder stile leads onto the railway embankment again.

Cross with care and locate the next ladder stile. This is the most difficult obstacle on the entire walk, including dodging trains on the ECML. This stile has certainly seen better days, so beware.

A time for regret

The path continues straight ahead. Not that there is much choice in the matter, for the dense foliage of Rushy Moor Plantation is on the left and the deep water of a ditch is on the right. In one or two places the path comes perilously close to the ditch. This is the moment when you regret the fourteenth pint at the Star.

About 250 metres from the railway, there is a bridge over the ditch to the right. Cross the bridge and go up the steps on the far side of the ditch. The view from the top of the steps marks a sudden return to urban life, with what seems to be an active rubbish tip on the right, surrounded by a metal fence. A broad track runs alongside the metal fence, passing the woodyard on the left. The track peters out to no more than a footpath and so reaches a bridge. Here you rejoin your outward route for the remainder of the walk back to the Askern pond and the car park. When the walk was being reconnoitred, we met one local lady who waxed eloquent about the beauty of Askern pond at sunset. She was right. A fitting end to a good walk.

2. Barnburgh

The Route: Barnburgh, Hickleton Road, Stables Lane, Barnburgh Cliff, Hangman Stone, St Helen's Lane, The Crown, Barnburgh.

Distance: 5km (3.1 miles)

Start: Coach and Horses GR 485033

Map(s): OS 1:25000 Pathfinder Series No. 716 Doncaster and Dearne.

How to get there:

By public transport: Daily bus services from Barnsley and Doncaster stop close to the Coach and Horses.

By car: This is not the easiest place to find, especially from the south. However, Barnburgh is signed from the A635 Doncaster to Barnsley road at Hickleton. This route will bring you to the cross roads in the centre of the village, by the Coach and Horses. There is no public car park, so please park tidily somewhere on the street.

The Walk

Of cats and men

Barnburgh is an ancient settlement, much added to following the sinking of the colliery in 1911. The church of St Peters is well worth a visit. In particular there is the fine effigy of the 15th century lord of the manor, Sir Percival Cresacre. He is depicted with his feet on a large cat and the church is known locally as the Cat and Man because of this. The tale is that he was attacked by this beast whilst returning home and was so severely mauled that he died of his injuries, but not before he had also killed the cat. Luckily such cats as roam the streets of Barnburgh nowadays do not seem to be so aggressive.

Heed the locals' warning

From the Coach and Horses pub in the centre of the village, turn right and go up Hickleton Road, passing the post office and shops on the right. Where the road bends to the left a footpath goes straight on, but you should ignore this. We met up with a fellow walker at this point, who gave us dire warnings about the steepness of the climb to Barnburgh Cliff and the muddiness of the track. In the latter respect at least he was accurate. Keep going along the road, passing the grandiose stables on the left. At the edge of the village there is a grand view to the left. Hoober Stand can be seen perched on its hilltop. It is amazing the number of view points where this monument features. Pass the Pinfold on the left, which was restored in the 1970s. Then look out for a bridleway sign on the right. This is Stables Lane. Turn right here and commence the ascent of Barnburgh Cliff.

The local warning about the mud soon becomes reality. Stables Lane is quite a rough little green road and where it does steepen, it is a question of one step forward and two back. The crags of Barnburgh Cliff can be seen ahead and to the right. When you are pausing for breath, look back across the valley, for the view is very extensive. The tower blocks on the south side of Sheffield were clearly visible, as were the Derwent Moors of the Peak District.

Continue upwards and where the track forks, go straight ahead. The track is a proper hedged green lane, but the surface was decidedly slippery and more than one of the author's companions found a soft landing after an incautious step. Eventually the track bears right and levels out at the top of the crags. There is a good view from here. Inevitably, dear old Hoober Stand can be seen, and Keppel's Column. Strangely though, you cannot see Conisbrough Castle. This is hidden by a shoulder of high land to the south.

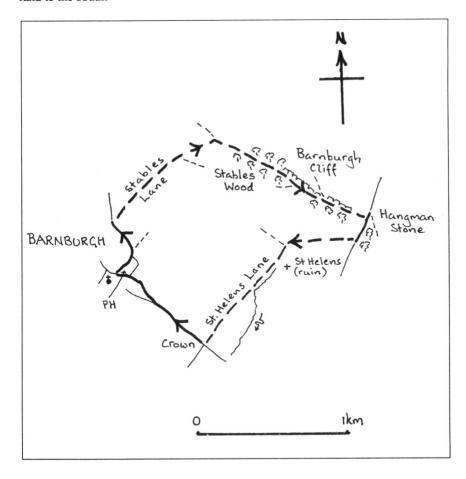

The view from the Crags

The path slants up to join the route along the crags. To the right now is Stables Wood, but to the left there is an extensive view. We counted four power stations and it is an interesting exercise trying to give names to them. There is a distant view of the A1(M), not too much of a distraction at this distance.

The track descends into the trees, then levels off at the foot of the crags. There is a wall on the right and an enormous view to the south. Ignore the footpath sign on the right. This will only take you back down into Barnburgh via an even more slippery route, according to our local informant. Instead, carry on along the track with the crags on the left. These look as if they have been quarried at some time, with the spoil being tipped down the hillside on the right. The track on which you are walking was presumably the means of access for carts. Continue ahead, ignoring the footpath sign on the left.

Where, Oh Where, is the Hangman Stone?

About 300 metres further on, you pass through a pair of gateposts and so reach the road. This is Hangman Stone Road. When we reconnoitred this walk we went left at this point, up to the top of the hill and then right, along a track for a short distance. We were hunting for the Hangman Stone which is marked on the map. Alas, there was nothing that was obviously a hangman's stone. Not a gibbet or rope in sight, so we retraced our steps to the road and turned left, down the hill.

The Coach and Horses

St Helen's Lane

Canter down the hill for about 200 metres, with a line of trees on the right. Where these finish, there is a bridleway sign and this is your route. Barnburgh church and the village can be clearly seen. Go along the bridleway, which is a broad track, but rough and pot-holed. This is St Helen's Lane. The track descends gently, accompanied by notices exhorting you not to deposit rubbish. The crags are to your right on the skyline. The track bears left and reaches a junction. Go straight on here. In the field on your left is a clump of trees. This marks the site of St Helen's chapel, now totally ruined and inaccessible. A stream runs down the left-hand side of the track for a short distance before it bears away to the left. St Helen's Lane rises over the shoulder of a low hill, before descending again quite sharply to reach the road opposite The Crown.

The Crown is another John Smiths pub, but it seems more given over to the car-borne visitor than the walker, so turn right here, along the road. Traffic moves fast along this road, but fortunately there is a footway on the right-hand side. As you approach Barnburgh, look to the right to see the octagonal dovecote on the hillside. This is one of the few remains of Barnburgh Hall, which was demolished by the Coal Board in 1969. Where the road forks, keep right, along the main route, but cross to take advantage of the footway. A few steps more, you round the corner and reach the Coach and Horses.

3. Bawtry

The Route: Bawtry, Bawtry viaduct, Bawtry Carr, Newington, Slaynes Lane, Misson, Bryans Close Lane, Rugged Carr Drain Bridge, Low Common Lane, Austerfield, Dam Bridge, Bawtry.

Distance: 11.25km (7 miles)

Start: Bawtry main street, by the Crown Hotel. GR 652931

Map(s): OS 1:25000 Pathfinder Series No. 728 Harworth and Gringley on the Hill.

How to get there:

By public transport: Daily bus services from Doncaster and Worksop, Retford and Gainsbro'. Frequent train service too, but alas, no station.

By car: As befits a town that boasts the Great North Road passing through the middle, Bawtry is well-served by class A roads. The A614, 631 and 638 all pass through, so you should have no difficulty in finding the place. The whole of the main street has parking on the west side. The starting point of the walk, the Crown Hotel, lies just north of the Tickhill road (A614)

The Walk

Of ports, pigs and Bawtry

The place name of Bawtry is first recorded in 1199 as "Baltry". The speculation is that this probably refers to a round shaped tree, from the Old English "ball and treow". However, on each of the approaches to the town there is a sign which proclaims Bawtry to be a 12th Century port. There is no doubt about this, but the sign designers somewhat understate the case, for there is evidence that Bawtry was a port in Roman times. Pigs of Derbyshire lead with Latin inscriptions have been found in the vicinity and the suggestion is that the metal was shipped along the River Idle to the Trent and thence to the continent. Sadly there is little left of the port except a few buildings and street names. Until 1974 the town was split in two by the county boundary. The west side of the Gt North Rd was in West Riding. The east was in Nottinghamshire. The joining of these two pieces of the same town was an unusual example of logic in the 1974 reorganisation of local government.

A problematical start

It has to be said that this walk is problematical. The author tried it twice. The first time he was lucky to survive a ducking in the flooded River Idle. The second time, he completed the walk, only to find that the "riverside" footpath on which he had walked had been nowhere near the line of the right of way, which turned out to be some few feet under water. A glance at the Pathfinder map will show a dotted green line, running alongside the River Idle in a north easterly direction from Bawtry. It was this that the author was attempting to follow. You will also notice that the green dots stop abruptly at a parish boundary. Clearly the path was the towpath alongside the Idle and must have been continuous, but the existence of a right of way is not proven. The walk described here recounts the author's route, but the section between Bawtry and Newington must be regarded with some suspicion. It is perfectly possible to walk to Newington along a roadside footway beside the A614 and then the lane signed to Misson. Until the right of way issue is sorted out, the road walk is the recommended route. Consult Nottingham County Council or Doncaster Metropolitan Borough Council before trying the riverside path.

Riverside antics

When the walk was reconnoitred, the author crossed the main road from the Crown and went down Church Walk, which is a tarred footpath. It runs between buildings to emerge on Church Street, almost opposite St Nicholas' church. We went left here and passed the church, which is not a very imposing building. When we reached Wharf Farm, there was a bridleway sign directing you to the right. This does not conform with the OS map which describes this path as a footpath. We followed the sign to a gate and stile, beyond which is the Bawtry viaduct. This ugly structure effectively cuts the town off from the river frontage. The railway carries a steady procession of express trains, for this is the East Coast Main Line. Beyond the viaduct the path turns left, through a muddy area.

The map indicates that the path follows the course of the river, but when the author first tried it, this section was under water. An obvious path keeps left, alongside the railway to reach a stile. This takes you into open fields, but about 150 metres west of the supposed right of way. On neither reconnoitre trip was the true right of way visible as it was flooded. However, there was a fairly obvious path bearing away to the right from the stile, heading towards the right-hand end of the hedge on the opposite side of the field. On the first visit, it would have been impossible to have gone any further to the right because of flooding. Even on the second visit it was only just possible to squeeze to the right of the hedge. It looked as if the locals kept just to the left of the hedge instead. At the end of this field the path was forced to the right by a barbed wire fence and hedge. In times of flood the "river" comes right up to this fence and it was here that the author nearly came to grief. There is a clearly walked path at this point, closely following the line of the fence and hedge, though it is fully 150 metres to the left of the mapped right of way. The floodlands to the right are a haven for all sorts of wildfowl. Many varieties of duck were seen, along with various gulls, swans and geese. Many times the author wished he had webbed feet, or preferably wings!

The path continued ahead with the fence to the left. Ahead we could discern Misson church tower, but there was an uncomfortable feeling that this distinct path bore little relationship to that shown on the map. Where the fence turned left, we carried straight on, across the field until we reached a ramshackle fence. A fenced track lead away to the left to a gate but this was of no use. The path carried on, through

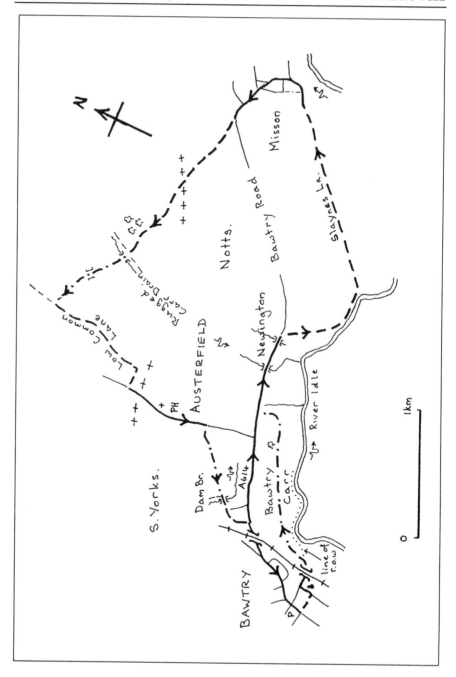

a gap in the fence, with the river now well to the right, beyond a line of thorns and alders. To the left were the gardens of houses on the A614 road. We met a number of locals out walking their dogs, one of whom advised us that the way to Newington lay to the left, just beyond the houses. Sure enough, a grassy track led left to a gate on top of the flood bank. The gate has a notice which says PRIVATE FISHING, but nothing about any path.

An unfortunate County Boundary

Here we joined the road route and turned right, towards Newington. It is quite possible and indeed preferable, to walk along the top of the flood bank, from which there is an extensive view. In view at this point is the Ship Inn at Newington – a grand pub, which has featured in a number of CAMRA guides.

Idling along

Go past the Ship, noting the Victorian letterbox as you go by. Pass the brick-built house just beyond the pub. This boasts a date of 1568, but that seems doubtful. There is no footway on the road beyond the pub, but fortunately this is only the road to Misson, so there's not too much traffic. About 400 metres beyond the pub, there is a turning to the right and a rough lane leads off towards the Idle. The river is hidden by the floodbank, which is soon reached. The lane rises to cross the flood barrier. On the right is the remains of a bridle gate, now clearly useless. The river is now in view ahead, along with a hill (!) on which sits the village of Everton. The Barrow Hills rise to a staggering 40 metres, a veritable mountain for these parts. Also on the far side of the river are what appear at first sight to be two black-clad fishermen, both with white scarves. On closer inspection these turn out to be connected with the drainage system and nothing to do with fishing at all. Nevertheless, you will encounter fishermen here, for now the lane runs alongside the river.

Nine Tailors' country

After about 200 metres the lane and the river part company again. The passage along the flood bank is closed by a gate, though there is a stile, despite no path being shown on the map. Ignoring both gate and stile, bear left, off the flood bank to reach another lane. This heads unerringly for Misson, which is now in view ahead, across a wide flat expanse of open land. Slaynes Lane is flat as the proverbial pancake and straight as a die for about 1.5 km. It has dikes either side, both water filled, but that on the right has the proportions of a canal and a number of bridges to suit. Misson church tower draws steadily nearer, but slowly. It is a wide view, only broken by the occasional willow tree and farmstead. "Nine Tailors' country" remarked the author's companion, and indeed devotees of Dorothy L Sayers novel would have felt at home here.

The otherwise peaceful approach to Misson was shattered at regular intervals by the roar of jet engines from the nearby Finningley airfield. On the only other occasion that the author has been to Misson, he witnessed the awe inspiring power of one of the RAF's Vulcan bombers taking off. A magnificent sight. A more devastating imposition on the landscape is in prospect, for there were notices advertising a proposal for an aggregates quarry.

At one time the dikes either side of Slaynes Lane must have been tree lined, but not now. There was evidence of recent felling and great piles of tree roots by the side of the track. After about 1.5 km the right-hand ditch swings suddenly to the right to join the Idle at a sluice. The lane bears left and passes a collection of railway van bodies. Hedges and fences now enclose the lane and soon the houses of Misson are reached. The lane, now a proper road, bends to the left. In the garden of the house just near the bend is a fine eucalyptus tree, an odd thing to find in this out of the way village. At the T-junction go straight ahead along West Street, noting the church to the right. If time permits, it is worth having a look around the church, then retracing your steps to this junction. West Street forks and here you go left, passing the Pinfold on the left. This is sadly in need of repair. West Street soon joins the Bawtry Road where a sign proclaims "Bawtry 3". For those desperate souls who feel they can go no further, there is a bus stop here.

Miss out on Misson Mill

Continue ahead, passing Misson Mill on the left. Do not expect an olde worlde water or wind mill. Misson Mill is a large modern agricultural building of little character and even less architectural charm. Pass by with ease and where the road bears left, go straight on, along a rough track. This is signposted as a footpath. This is Bryans Close Lane, a name to stir the hearts of all true Yorkshiremen, but sadly nothing to do with the great cricketer. The land on either side of the lane has been quarried for aggregates and now largely restored, though at a lower level. Any lingering hopes you might have of spotting the remains of the erstwhile Misson branch line are quickly dispelled for it has vanished as if it had never been. Away to the left can be seen the headgear of Harworth colliery. Keep left at the fork in the track, noting the obviously disobeyed sign saying "No Dumping". Suddenly, on the left, there are the tell tale double hedges of the course of the old railway. Only briefly do they appear before vanishing again.

Below sea level

Another fork in the track, where again you keep left, through the gateposts. The track now narrows to little more than footpath width as it runs alongside a hedge. A small oak woodland is passed on the right. Careful inspection will reveal that there are beehives in the wood, which are best left severely alone. Just beyond the wood a track goes off to the left, but you should ignore this. About 100 metres further on you reach another track at a T-junction, not shown on the OS map. There is a new pond and planting to the right, again, not on the OS map. A footbridge leads across the deep cut of Rugged Carr Drain and the line of the path continues ahead with another deep ditch to the right. Austerfield village can be seen to the left. The ditch marks the boundary between South Yorkshire and Nottinghamshire. Look out for the boundary stone, with the M for Misson on it at the point where the Austerfield Drain goes off to the right. The map shows that at this point you stand 3 metres above sea level. By that reckoning, the bottom of Austerfield Drain is probably below sea level!

Continue alongside the ditch, the far side of which is overgrown with scrub. Soon another footbridge is reached and crossed and the path continues ahead, skirting the field. On the right is a golf course. To the left, stony fields. At the end of the field the path emerges onto a green lane and here you go left. You will have noticed the steady climb from the boundary stone for you now stand at 7 metres above sea level. Proceed along Low Common Lane, which is hedged right and left. Misson church and the mill can be glimpsed through the trees on the left. An area of new planting is soon reached on the right. For some reason the new trees are conifers, which look quite out of place. The lane twists its way between the hedges until it swings sharp right by another collection of railway van bodies. These are just about on the course of the old Misson branch line. The track now climbs quite sharply to reach the main road, which stands proudly at 10 metres above sea level. Here you go left into Austerfield.

Austerfield village

Austerfield is recorded as early as the 8th century, when it was the centre of an ecclesiastical dispute. The villages most famous son is Wm. Bradford, who was lived at Austerfield Manor. The house is still extant and William's name appears in the baptismal records for 1589. He sailed to America in 1620 and became Governor of the new colony of Plymouth. A plaque in the church records that he was the first democratically elected governor in America. Needless to say, the village is much visited by Americans, eager for their country's historical roots.

Follow the main road, sticking to the footway. Just beyond the Austerfield Field Study Centre, the railway used to cross the road, but you'd never know. There is a nice development of new cottages in a traditional style on the left, before you reach St Helen's church. This tiny church is well set back from the road. The present church dates back to the 11th century and still retains many Norman features, including the font. The dragon carving over the doorway is thought to be rather older than the main body of the church and may even date back to the Saxon period. Worth a look round if you have time. A short distance further on is the Mayflower pub; from here, go left and continue along the main road. Ignore the first footpath sign on the right and continue ahead until you reach the last house on the left. Just opposite the bus shelter, there is another footpath sign on the right. This points up a narrow track, between buildings. After a very short distance, just before the bungalow, the path veers away to the left, across an area shown on the map as "pits (disused)". In practice this is just an area of rough ground and the path across it is clear underfoot. It does not follow the left-hand boundary as might be expected, but clips the left-hand corner of the field to reach a stile. The stile is hidden from the bungalow by a slight change in ground level, but it cannot be missed. Once over the stile, follow the hedge on the right to another stile by a gate. This is Dam Bridge, though neither dam nor bridge are particularly obvious. To the right is a riding school. The presence of horses in this field, combined with wet weather, made the passage of this stile an interesting experience!

Back to Bawtry

Once over the stile go straight on, along the lane, which soon swings to the left as it comes up against the railway line. No Misson branch this, for here you rejoin the East Coast Main Line. Before the railway was built, this lane carried straight on. The continuation still exists, now known as Station Road. Some of Bawtry's station buildings still remain, but no trains stop here now, which must be galling for the local residents. Continue beside the line for a short distance, until the main A614 is reached. Go right here and follow the main road under the railway bridge, past the Station Hotel (Whitbread) and the Phoenix (Theakstons) back into the town centre.

4. Bolsterstone

The Route: Bolsterstone Church, Heads Lane, Low Flat Farm, Hunger Hill Farm, The Height, Wind Hill Farm, Long Lane, Mucky Lane, Heads Lane, Bolsterstone Church.

Distance: 7.5km (4.7 miles)

Start: Bolsterstone Church GR 271968

Map(s): OS 1:25000 Pathfinder Series No. 726, Sheffield (N) and Stocksbridge

How to get there:

By public transport: There is a Monday to Saturday service from Sheffield and Stocksbridge to Bolsterstone.

By car: Many and devious are the ways to Bolsterstone. The most obvious is to use the A616 to Deepcar crossroads (A616/B6088), then go left, if coming from the south, or right, if coming from the north. Ascend the hill through the housing estates, out into open country and thus into Bolsterstone. The village is signed at the cross roads. There is limited parking on the road in front of the church or village hall.

The Walk

Bolsterstone village

Bolsterstone is a lovely village, on the edge of the Peak National Park. It is perched on the top of the steep scarp overlooking the Ewden Valley in which lie Broomhead and More Hall Reservoirs. The village has a macabre name that belies its tranquillity nowadays. According to the Dictionary of English Place names "Bolstyrston" means "the stone on which criminals were beheaded". If you see anyone striding purposefully towards you swinging an axe, run.

Despite its bloodthirsty origins, Bolsterstone is now a picturesque spot, with stone built cottages clustered round those two founts of village life, the pub and the church. The present church is a 19th century rebuild, but there has been one on this site since the 12th century. The churchyard contains some interesting relics of earlier times, including two large stones which are thought to belong to a now vanished prehistoric stone circle.

From the church go right, along the lane signed as a No Through Road. This is Heads Lane. There are glimpses to the left down into the valley of the Ewden Beck. To the right is the church yard. As you leave the village behind the true nature of Heads Lane is revealed. It is a fine ridge top route, with extensive views to either side. It pursues an unerring course towards the pointed hill seen ahead. This is The Height. The view to the left includes Broomhead Reservoir, the upper of the two

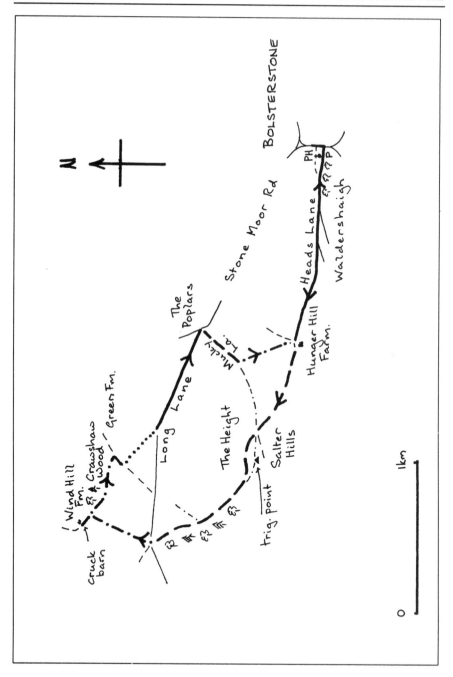

reservoirs in this valley. However, the view is much more extensive than the Ewden Valley only, as it encompasses a wide swathe of the eastern Peak District moors. The nonsensical nature of local government boundaries becomes clear when you realise that the land on the right-hand side of the lane is outside the National Park, whereas the land on the left is inside.

Waldershaigh

The lane continues gently past Waldershaigh House to the left and then past the driveway to Waldershaigh Cottage. Ignore the path leading off steeply downhill to the left and carry on along the lane. The lane passes Low Flat Farm and then narrows appreciably, beginning to rise towards Hunger Hill. At Hunger Hill Farm the tarmac road ends at twin gates and ladder stiles. The more intelligent amongst you will now have realised that this is a tadpole walk, in that the section you have just walked has to be rewalked in the opposite direction on the return journey. That being the case, you could have brought your car to this point and saved nearly one and a half miles overall. This would of course be cheating, and in any case there's hardly room at this point to swing a cat, let alone park a car.

An inaccessible trig point

Go over the left-hand ladder stile and out onto open moor. A drystone wall to the left blocks out most of the view in that direction, but the view to the right is extensive. Stocksbridge can be clearly seen with Hunshelf Bank behind. The track continues upwards, sometimes roughly paved with setts or bricks. It is worth pausing every now and then to look over the wall on the left to the Ewden Valley and Broomhead Moors. It comes as a surprise to see a small fenced enclosure on the far side of the wall. This seems to house a rain gauge. The track now forks on the approach to Salter Hills, a name deeply redolent of the ancient trade in Cheshire salt. One track goes off sharply back to the right, another bears away left, descending to Salter Hills. A third route carries straight on, through the right-hand gateway, which is waymarked. This is your route. Immediately beyond the gateway a narrow path bears away left, through a gap in the wall, heading uphill towards the trig point on top of The Height. Unfortunately this is not a right of way so you are deprived of a fine view from the summit. Instead, carry on beside the wall and climb steadily up the hill until the summit point is tantalisingly close on the left. It is still out of bounds, despite the numerous gaps in the wall. Follow the path through the bilberry, heather and bracken until you reach a small wood on the left. The path twists and turns through the tussocks of grass and around trees which have escaped the confining wall. The ground underfoot is decidedly spongy in places and bearing in mind that this walk was reconnoitred after a long dry spell, you could normally look forward to a muddy passage.

A fine cruck barn

Ignore the paths going off left into the wood and right, across the moor towards the road. Instead, carry on alongside the wood and the wall until you too reach the road. This is Long Lane. Cross the road and go straight on, over the signposted stile, back into fields again. The small fields on the left betoken a considerable struggle to farm this rough upland. On the right the large field is but one step removed from moorland and seems to be rapidly reverting to its natural state. Follow the left-hand wall down the field to a gate in the bottom left-hand corner. Your route goes right here, alongside the wood, but it is worth first deviating through the gate on the left to Wind Hill Farm. As you pass through the next gate which takes you into the farm complex, note the barn on the left. It is a good example of a cruck barn, though urgently in need of restoration. The restored barn on the right might also be a cruck barn as well, but it is difficult to be certain without being able to see inside. Retrace your steps to the gate by the wood and go straight on, with the wood to your left. The wood is a delightful mixture of holly, birch and oak, rather than the overpowering conifers.

Views of Stocksbridge

At the end of the wood, the sketchy path continues to follow the wall on the left, with a view ahead to Stocksbridge. Where the wall tends to the left there is a stile in the corner of the field. Go over this and continue alongside the left-hand wall. Underbank Reservoir can be seen below to the left. This reservoir was one of a series built by Sheffield Corporation Waterworks in the 19th century in the tributary valleys of the River Don. Not for nothing is the area to the north west of the city known as Sheffield's Lake District. Go through the next stile or its adjacent gateway and cross the next field to another stile by a signpost. It is tempting to head across this field to an obvious gateway but the stile lies to the left of the gate. The stile leads out onto a track and here you go right. Climb the track, passing the tempting gate referred to above and then go through another gate on the left, just before the solitary rowan. In this field, follow the wall on the left, bearing slightly right to reach a stile in the far wall, just to the right of the corner. Pass through this stile into another field. Field boundaries have been removed here, and the map is inaccurate. The left-hand wall takes a sharp kink to the left and here the "path", which is not obvious on the ground at all, bears right to cross the field diagonally. Bolsterstone Church is in view ahead and is a good marker. In the southeastern corner of the field (far right), there is a stile and signpost marking the exit onto the road. This is again Long Lane and here you go left.

Of by-passes and Mucky Lanes

From Long Lane there is a good view across to the infamous Stocksbridge By-Pass. So much for the Department of Transport landscaping its new roads. Stocksbridge and its famous steel works nestle down in the valley bottom. Go along the bilberry-lined lane, noting the spring on the right. Just before the road junction there is an ancient car in an equally old garage on the left. At the road junction go right, but not along the road. Instead, head up the narrow rough lane. This is Mucky Lane, an ill omened name. The first section is not too bad, with little muck. At the stile in the fence across the lane, the nature of the track changes. Beyond the stile the path deserts the lane which now is decidedly damp, and runs just to the right, on the drier moor.

The map shows the right of way remaining in the lane, between the walls, but this is clearly not the walked route.

At the next stile the walled lane ceases and the path forks. Take the left-hand route, over the stile, then up the field with the wall on your right. The path climbs to a big ladder stile in the top corner of the field. Negotiate this obstacle to arrive back at Hunger Hill Farm and Heads Lane. From here you should need no description of the route back, but you can vary your outward route by walking through the churchyard to emerge at the lych gate near the stocks. The Castle Inn is just to the left.

5. Cannon Hall Country Park

The Route: Cannon Hall Country Park, Cawthorne village, Barnby Hall, Barnby Green Farm, Lower Norcroft Farm, Banks Hall, Tansand Beck Bridge, Clough Green, Cannon Hall CP.

Distance: 8.25km (5.1 miles)

Start: Cannon Hall Country Park GR 079273, for car users. The car park is pay and display, costing 60p for 2 hours, 80p up to 4 hours. No parking on the roadside, which has double yellow lines. Bus stop near Spencer Arms for public transport devotees.

Map(s): OS 1:25000 Pathfinder Series No. 715 Barnsley and Penistone

How to get there:

By public transport: daily bus services to Huddersfield and Barnsley.
By car: the A635 Barnsley to Oldham road skirts Cawthorne village. The country park is signed about 500 metres west of the village.

The Walk

Cannon Hall and its geese

From the car park, make your way down to the lake, avoiding the Canada Geese as best you can. At the lake turn left and follow the water's edge to the first weir and bridge. There is a view to the left from here, up to the hall. This was the country seat of the Spencer-Stanhope family until 1951 when it was sold to Barnsley Borough Council. It is also the regimental museum of the 13/18 Royal Hussars. Do not cross the bridge, but carry on along the north bank of the cascade. The tower of Cawthorne church can be seen to the right. Pass another weir and a propped up yew tree to reach a second bridge. This you cross, taking care to avoid the spiked railings.

Into Cawthorne village

Beyond the bridge a tarred path runs straight ahead to a gate and signpost. Carry on, through the gate, heading towards the church tower. The track you are on soon goes through another gate and emerges onto the road in the midst of a fairly new residential development. Continue ahead, noting the grindstone tastefully positioned on your left. A pair of stone gateposts by the old house guard the junction with the main road. Here you go left. Although it is not obvious from the map, there is a stream on your left just below the road. Pass the Cawthorne Club on the left and then cross the road and bear right up the church access. This is a pleasant, tree lined avenue, which leads steadily up to the ornamental gateway into the churchyard. On the left is the faded grandeur of the Stanhope memorial. The church itself dates back to the 13th century and is dedicated to All Saints. Perhaps surprisingly for those without much knowledge of ecclesiastical boundaries, this parish forms part of the Diocese of Wakefield.

Skirt round to the left of the church, passing the gardener's hut. Then bear right, to reach Church Lane. Here go left and thus reach the main road again. The Spencer Arms is just to your left, on the opposite side of the road. On your right is an old milepost from turnpike days, now marooned in the middle of a triangle of roads. There is an intricately-carved fountain and a seat commemorating the winning of the Best Kept Village competition in 1988. This is a well-deserved title.

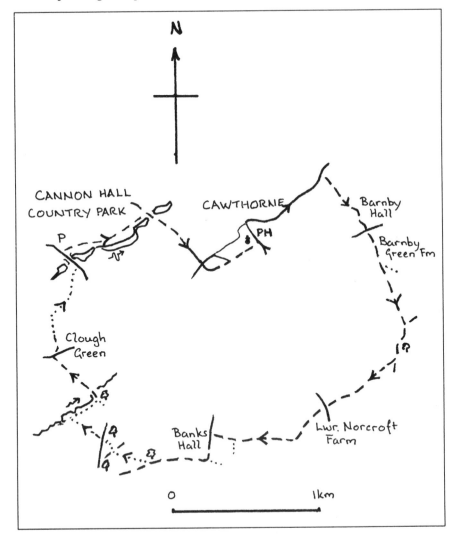

The Spencer Arms

From the Spencer Arms pub, turn right and walk down to the T-junction. Turn right, along the road signed to Darton and Kexbrough, passing the Post Office and the house with the cross carved in the wall. As you walk down the Kexbrough road you pass the chapel and pottery on the left and a well, with an 1881 date stone, on your right. Ignore the bridleway sign on your left and continue along the road for a further 250 metres. Beware the fact that beyond Clay Hall there is no footway, but there is what appears at first glance to be a Peak Park boundary sign! This turns out to be the Cawthorne village sign. Perhaps they have aspirations to be in the National Park. Barnsley Borough please note. There is a good view to the left from here, over the valley of the Cawthorne Dike to Kexbrough and beyond. About 100 metres beyond Clay Hall, look out for a footpath sign and stile on the right, for this is your route.

Barnby Hall

Negotiate the stile and follow the path alongside the fence, on the right-hand side of the field. As the path rises steadily there is a good view to the right, back over Cawthorne village. Barnby Hall can be seen ahead and this is your next objective. To the left is the M1 in all its glory, with Barnsley beyond. As you approach Barnby Hall, bear right to the gate, then go straight on, between the buildings to reach the A635.

Cross the A635 with care and go down the track opposite. This leads to Barnby Green Farm. The footpath passes through the farm complex, skirting to the left of the barn. The path continues, with a fence on the left, until you pass through a gateway, which is waymarked. Here an obvious track bears away to the left, but your route lies straight ahead, across the field. Make for the left-hand end of the line of trees. The only marker en route is a trough in the middle of the field. Do not get so besotted with the view of the M1 that you deviate off route. Hopefully you should find a waymarked stile at the end of the trees. This drops you into another field. Proceed down the right-hand side of the field by the fence, until you reach a stile in the corner. This leads onto a narrow, fenced green lane, very pleasant, with trees either side.

Burglar alarms and waymarks

Soon the lane runs alongside a strip of woodland and crosses a small stream. Beware the gnarled tree roots which seem to be placed deliberately to trip the unwary or inebriated walker! At the end of the wood there is a distinct crossing of tracks. Here you go right, passing through either the waymarked stile or the gate, back into open fields again. Bear left in the field, to a gateway by the ash tree. This too is waymarked. (The gateway, not the ash tree). In this next field there is no obvious path and the land form is such that you cannot see the far side. You can see a house with a chimney, lying between two clumps of trees. Head for the house, making a bee-line across the field. Part way across you will be reassured by the sight of a prominent yellow waymark on the bungalow now seen ahead. This turns out to be a burglar alarm box, but it is a good marker nevertheless. You will also notice a tree-lined track which fringes the field on your right. As the right-hand boundary gets closer, you will spot numerous gaps in the tree line, any of which will take you onto the track. It is not at all clear where the path should join this track. There is no way mark or sign of any description, but close study of the map would indicate that the track should be joined about 150 metres before the house. Only an oak and ash tree mark this spot. No stile or gate or sign. Carry on past the house to reach Silkstone Lane.

Cross the lane and go through the stile by the signpost. There is a yellow waymark on the electricity pole, but it would be difficult to go wrong here anyhow. Keep the fence to your left and skirt round Lower Norcroft Farm to reach a stile in the wall on the left. Here you enter open fields again and the path ahead is not obvious. Head down the field, to the right of the clump of trees. You should spot a waymark on a post. The stream shown on the map is culverted, so no problem there. Skirt the trees, which stand on the edge of quite a steep bank on your left, and make your way up the other half of the field, to a stile in the right-hand corner. Go over the stile and keep close company with the hedge on your left, until it does the inevitable kink right and left. The path keeps straight on, passing through a gap in the hedge, so that the hedge is now to your right. Banks Hall is now in view ahead.

Banks Hall and flies

Keep alongside the hedge in order to find a well-hidden stile in the corner. Find a way over this and carry on alongside the right-hand hedge. Cawthorne church tower is in view to the right. A stile at the end of the field leads onto a lane and here you turn left. Follow the lane up to the gateway to Banks Hall, now an old people's home. The map seems to imply that the path goes through the gate and the grounds, but this is not the case. Just by the entrance to Banks Hall there is a stile on the left. This takes you back into the field you have recently left!. Now go right, following the ornate boundary wall of Banks Hall gardens, until you reach a stile by a gate.

Here disaster struck the author. As he passed through the gate, he was surrounded by a cloud of those tiny, slow-flying black insects, one of which decided to settle in his eye. This resulted in the second hospital visit in the course of researching this book. Indeed the hospital visit took longer than the walk. Beware flies and see the Low Bradfield walk for further medical adventures.

Having checked that the coast is clear of flies, pass through the stile and proceed along the broad track at the back of Banks Hall. The hall itself can be seen just to the right. Not a very spectacular building. At the next gate and stile go right, as if you were about to enter the grounds. In a very short distance there is a gate, before which your track swings to the left, to run as a walled track alongside a wood. Follow this track, noting the new windmills in view ahead and the clay pits on the far side of the valley to your left. At the end of the wood there is the inevitable gate and stile. The track continues ahead, but your route lies to the right, over another stile in the fence and thus into the field. In the field there is no sign of a path at all. Head diagonally left, rising across the field, making for the middle of the belt of trees seen ahead. With a bit of luck, or you can call it good navigation, you will locate a stile in the corner of the field, no waymarkers or signs though. The stile leads into the belt of trees, through which the path twists and winds. When you reach a crossing of paths, go straight on, following the path's every turn, some of which are waymarked, until you emerge on the road at a gap in the hedge.

Variations on a brickworks theme

Cross over the road to a stile, from which steps lead down into a thin belt of trees. There is a magnificent view of the brick works from this point! Pass through the trees to another stile and thus into open fields. Follow the hedge on your right, down the field to the triangle of trees in the corner. Here there is another stile, but beyond this there is no semblance of a path. This field is a large one, and a glance at the map will show the path heading straight down the field towards the brook in the bottom. At one time, pre brick works, the path seems to have crossed the brook and headed straight on towards Clough Green. Now you simply go down the field until you reach the waymarker post at the bottom and there turn right. Follow the fence, stream and myriad waymarks, to reach a stile in the corner of the field. You will by now have realised that you could have made a bee-line for this stile by cutting diagonally across the field from the point where you entered it. There is some evidence that this does happen, but this is not the right of way and is not the suggested route.

Clamber over the rickety stile into the wood. Almost at once, a path joins from the right. Soon after the path forks. This is not shown on the map. Go left here and descend the steps to reach the bridge over the Tansand Beck. The use of the word "beck" for a stream is reminiscent of the Lake District and indicative of Norse influence.

The home of Magna Carta?

Climb up from the stream to a stile, which takes you back into fields again. Follow the hedge on your right, ignoring the brickworks on your left. As you pass through a gateway the path levels out and Clough Green is seen ahead, along with Cannon Hall and Cawthorne church away to the right. At Clough Green a gate and stile lead into a short green lane between the buildings and thus onto the main A635 road. One of the houses rejoices in the historic name of Runnymede, but any resemblance between this area and the famous island in the Thames is purely coincidental.

Cross the road, noting the fine turnpike milestone, and negotiate the gate or stile by the signpost. Follow the track for a short distance, then, as you near the barn, go left over a stile into fields again. Follow the fence cum hedge on the left, which skirts the horse training area on your right. There have been field boundaries *added* here, so the map is wrong. At the next stile continue straight on alongside the fence and hedge. You are now beginning the descent to the valley of Cawthorne Dike, which at this point has a different name. According to the map it is called the Daking Brook.

The next stile is an awkward double affair, but reasonably agile walkers should have no problem. Straight on, still alongside the hedge, to another stile. Once over this, bear right, going diagonally across the field, heading for the right-hand end of the clump of trees. There is no obvious path on the ground, but reassuringly there is a stile and a waymark as you reach the fence near the trees. Go straight on at this point, skirting round to the right of the houses. Beyond the houses the path swings left to cross the access track, then makes a bee-line down the field, heading just to the right of the house with the twisted chimneys. As you approach the house you will see it carries a date of 1856. Of more significance to you at this point however, is the location of the stile which gets you out of this field. It is not, as you might have expected, in the corner of the field, but in the bottom hedge, near the house. Having found and negotiated the stile go right, until you reach the road. Here turn left and make your way back, over the Cascade Bridge, to the car park at Cannon Hall.

6. Conisbrough

The Route: Doncaster station, Doncaster Lock, Don Navigation, Newton Lane, Sprotbrough Lock, Sprotbrough Flash Nature Reserve, Conisbrough viaduct, Consibrough station.

Distance: 10.25km (6.4 miles)

Start: Doncaster station. GR 572032

Map(s): OS 1:25000 Pathfinder Series No. 716, Doncaster and Dearne and 727, Rotherham.

How to get there:

By public transport: The walk starts at Doncaster station which is well-served by trains from all over the place. Conisbrough has a frequent daily train service from Sheffield, Rotherham and Doncaster. There are also various daily bus services which pass the station.

By car: Given the need to use the train at some point in this walk, it seems almost nonsensical to suggest a means of access by car. If you do insist on using a car you will first have to find Conisbrough. This is not difficult as it lies on the A630 trunk road between Doncaster and Rotherham. The station lies down in the valley bottom, past the Castle, just off the A6023. By July 1995, when the first phase of the Earth Centre opens, there will presumably be signs directing you to the site, which is adjacent to the station.

The Walk

Finding your way out of Doncaster

Catch the train from Conisbrough to Doncaster and alight there. From the main exit of the station, turn left, along the road and walk to the roundabout. Here go left. The road rises to cross first the railway line and then the canal. This is North Bridge, which used to carry the Great North Road, or A1. Thankfully the A1 no longer passes through the middle of Doncaster, though North Bridge is still unbelievably busy. You will meet the present A1 later in the walk.

Just over the canal, turn left and descend the steps or ramp to reach the towpath of the Don Navigation at Doncaster Lock. The lock is half buried under the road and railway bridges, which means that it is like operating in a tunnel. However, your route lies in the opposite direction, away from the hustle and bustle of North Bridge. Note that not all towpaths are public rights of way, though this section is. Later on in this walk there are sections of path which are only permissive. You must respect British Waterways' right to close these, especially for maintenance purposes.

The towpath soon rises to cross a bridge over an arm of the canal, in which there are a few moored boats. Most of them do not seem to have moved for some considerable time, a sad reflection on modern freight transport methods. At the far end of the arm the canal ends abruptly in a weir. Continue along the towpath, which is well-kept with a decent surface and fresh planting, a credit to the town. The search lights are a bit disconcerting though. Perhaps the new building on the right isn't a power station which is what the author's map says it is! Immediately beyond the new building, the towpath abruptly narrows and becomes a muddy path with the usual tangle of canalside vegetation. On the far side of the canal is the former Great Northern Railway Company's locomotive works, the famous Doncaster Plant. From these workshops came such famous engines as Flying Scotsman and the world record holder for steam, Mallard.

Don Navigation and Cusworth Hall

The canal bends to the right and reaches a curious twin bridge over the river. The lower and wider of the two structures seems to be the towpath, for horses. The other seems to be the footpath, but why two were required is a mystery. The bridges span the River Don, which leaves the canal at this point, to make its own way through the town that bears its name. Beyond the bridges the towpath continues across open fields, with a wholly rural feel, though you are only a kilometre from the traffic of North Bridge. On the hillside to the right you can see Cusworth Hall now part of a country park. The present house dates back to 1740 when the then owner Wm Wrightson decided to vacate his Elizabethan manor house and have a modern home constructed. Both buildings still exist. Many of the buildings in the village are of limestone. The earliest record of the village appears in Domesday in 1086. Curiously, the church in the village is not Church of England but Orthodox, largely as a result of the stipulations of a will, which prevented the last member of the Wrightson family becoming Roman Catholic. Denied this option and spurning the C of E, the last of the Wrightsons chose Orthodoxy instead.

The path keeps close to the riverbank and soon reaches a stile in a fence. An obvious path runs away to the right towards a green gate to the right of the farm buildings. However, this is not your route. Instead keep on top of the flood bank and head towards the left of the buildings. There scarcely seems to be any room between the house and the river, but as you approach you will spot a stile. This leads onto a narrow path which squeezes its way twixt water and wall.

Where you emerge from the confines of the river and wall, the path swings right and climbs away from the river bank to join a wide track. Keep left here, and where the track bears away from the river, descend to the left to rejoin the riverbank at a stile. (The map shows two parallel footpaths at this point). Pass through a small area of woodland which fringes the river. A series of stiles takes the path through the wood and a scrubby area, a little way from the riverbank, then out into open fields again, with the main flow of the river away to the left. Turn left at this point and follow the flood bank round the great sweep of Hexthorpe bend. Hexthorpe lies on the opposite bank of the river, along with the main Sheffield to Doncaster railway line. The side containing the path is wholly rural. The path is easy to follow, with only a couple of stiles to obstruct the march. To the right, after the second stile there

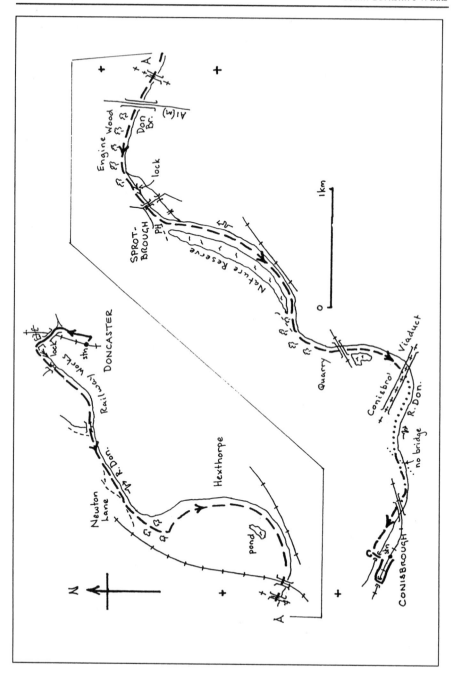

is a pond, probably the last remnant of a former course of the Don, but now a haven for wildfowl.

Early Doncaster by-passes

The first of a succession of bridges is now in view, this one carrying the Doncaster North avoiding line. This was built to carry coal trains destined for the Humber ports, round Doncaster, without cluttering up the main station area. An early Doncaster By-pass in fact.

As you approach the railway bridge you pass over a sluice. Which way does the water go through this sluice? Is it designed to relieve the Don by allowing water onto the low lying meadows, or is it to drain the flooded meadows? It is difficult to distinguish. Be careful if you are gazing in rapture at the lattice girders of the railway bridge, or you'll run head first into a fence. Better use the stile provided.

Pass under the railway bridge and you are at once confronted by another. This is a much more austere affair as befits the lateness of its construction and the impecunious companies that built it. This line too was built to carry coal round Doncaster, but the builders had even more grandiose ideas. They envisaged passenger traffic too, and even went to the expense of building stations, including a site at Doncaster. In the event no passenger service was ever put on and so the stations were never used. As the line duplicated others in the area it has long since closed, but a flight of steps on the right leads up to the embankment. The route is now used by walkers, but you should keep on the river bank and head towards the third bridge. This carries the A1(M) over the Don. It is a massive concrete structure, much larger than the two railway viaducts, and it carries a steady procession of car and lorries. Down at river level the noise is not too intrusive, but it can be heard over quite a long distance.

A stile takes the path under the A1 and reveals a surprise. This is not one bridge, but two close together. Between the two the safety conscious Department of Transport have hung wire mesh, just in case anyone is daft enough to leap over the central barrier. Just beyond the A1 bridge another flight of steps leads away to the right towards Sprotbrough. Again these are ignored.

Sprotbrough

Almost inevitably, Sprotbrough was mentioned in Domesday, but the greatest single influence probably came from the long association with the Copley family, who owned the village for over four hundred years. The Hall was demolished in 1926 and the site redeveloped, but the village still retains the air of an estate village. The church is certainly over 800 years old and has a number of interesting features. Well worth a visit if you have the time and inclination to leave the canal for a while.

Sprotbrough Lock

Continue along the riverside path, through the woodland, with limestone cliffs on the right. This area is shown on the map as Engine Wood. The river bends gently to the left and soon the A1 viaduct slips out of view and out of hearing. Now you can see Sprotbrough Lock ahead. The path veers away from the riverbank, crossing the lock overflow and a sluice with some ancient machinery on the right, before climbing and rejoining the canal again. This is one of the locks which was fairly recently rebuilt, deepened and lengthened to take bigger boats. Maintenance work was in progress when the author passed this way, so no boats were passing through, but there were a few big working boats moored. The towpath dives under the road bridge carrying the Sprotbrough to Warmsworth road over the canal and river.

Beyond the bridge, the towpath runs parallel with a road and soon reaches the Boat Inn. This is a most tempting hostelry, where it is easy to linger and probably forget that you are some way from your destination. Leaving with regret, resume your course along the canal towpath, which is signposted and here is a public right of way. A couple of hundred metres from the inn, the canal rejoins the river and at about the same point you come to the start of Sprotbrough Flash Nature Reserve. This is on your right, and consists of a lake, over a kilometre long, formed by subsidence. It now looks wholly natural and is a haven for bird life. The towpath squeezes its way between the lake and the river. Even on such a narrow strip of land as this the fishermen find space to pitch. One prize trio were busily disentangling their lines, with one member of the group pouring water from his wellingtons. When asked if he'd fallen in, he exclaimed that it was just sweat!

The Boat Inn

Sprotbrough Flash

On the opposite side of the river is the railway and an active quarry, but neither detract from the walk. After about half a kilometre along the reserve, there is a path off to the right. This leads to a hide, from which the fascinating antics of the birds can be observed. We were surprised to see three cormorants, busily drying their wings on the artificial perches in the middle of the lake. These birds are normally regarded as seaside residents, so we thought their presence so far inland was unusual. It seems as if cormorants, like gulls, have begun to move inland. After watching the cormorants, the gulls and the great crested grebes for a while, we reluctantly moved on. Leaving the hide, return to the towpath and go right.

Soon the end of the reserve is reached and you pass through a gate into a wooded area. There is a seat here but you surely cannot need any more rests. As you enter the wood, there is a glimpse to the left along the valley to Conisbrough viaduct. The path emerges abruptly from the wood into a pile of jumbled boulders, which fringe an active limestone quarry. The path climbs slightly away from the river and crosses over the access to a tipping dock, where boats were loaded with limestone. The map indicates a fork in the path at this point, but it is not obvious. Keep on the beaten track, which soon descends nearer to the river again and passes under the bridge which carries the Sheffield to Doncaster railway.

Conisbrough viaduct

Keep alongside the river, heading almost due south at this point. Soon the river takes a bend towards the south west and the great Conisbrough viaduct comes into view, with the castle framed by one of the arches. The viaduct is a massive structure, consisting of 21 arches plus a 150ft central lattice girder span. Its maximum height above river level is 113ft. It was built primarily for coal traffic as part of the Dearne Valley Railway in the early part of this century. Passenger traffic was rather an afterthought and the stations consisted of little more than raised areas of earth on which was plonked a redundant coach body. Needless to say this service was neither profitable nor long lived. The entire line closed in 1966.

The path continues by the river, with the viaduct drawing steadily nearer and looking more impressive at every step. Access to the viaduct is not possible now, but some years ago the author ventured over it. The point that sticks most in his memory was the open access-way into the lattice girder span. From there a rusty ladder led down to the lower girders, with nothing below except the Don. Further investigation was deemed unwise.

Pass below the viaduct and the obvious path seems to end abruptly. A semblance of route continues round the left-hand side of the field, with the river hidden from view by scrub and trees. At the far end of the field, the path reappears as it passes through an area of scrub. Beyond the scrub there is a view over to the castle, perched on its hilltop. The path sticks close to the river, passes over a stile and is then hemmed in by the railway line, above and on the right. An area of rough and boggy ground is now reached, across which various paths meander, each seeking to gain a more sensible foothold.

Those of you studying the map will be alarmed to find that none of the paths head for the river, as indicated. Neither is there any sign of a bridge, though apparently there was one once a ferry and there are proposals for its reinstatement. Continue ahead, making for the point where the railway crosses the river. The paths converge to cross a stone culvert in the middle of the "field" and then continue towards the railway bridge.

Instability threatens walkers

As you reach the railway bridge, there is a sign which proclaims "Unstable bank, proceed at own risk". This is a fine time to tell of these problems, for the only alternative is to backtrack to Sprotbrough and cross the river there. The author, who is already unstable anyway, decided to proceed. There was a small length where the path had fallen into the river and where the bank did indeed look worse for wear. However, it seemed as if work was being done to remedy the situation, so hopefully there will be no problems by the time this book is published. Check with British Waterways just to make sure. The path passes under the railway bridge, the piers of which seem to have an alarming lean on them. Perhaps there should be a sign on Conisbrough station similar to that on the canal bank.

The towpath beyond this point has obviously had a lot of work done on it as part of the reclamation works surrounding the former colliery, which is being redeveloped as part of the Earth Centre project. The first phase is due to open in July 1995 connecting the site directly with the railway station, so the next two paragraphs will rapidly become outdated.

Two bridges are quickly reached. Both served the colliery. Pass under both and then immediately on the right is a flight of steps. These lead up to the footbridge. A sign proclaims that the bridge is private, but this relates to the former colliery. Certainly no-one made any attempt to stop the author or his companion using the bridge and there were plenty of people doing likewise. Alternatively one could use the other bridge, which carried the access road to the colliery.

[The bridge over the Don belongs to the Earth Centre from whom permission for its use should be sought: Earth Centre Project, Kilner's Bridge, Doncaster Road, Denaby Main, Doncaster DN12 4DY.]

Safely over the Don there is the final choice of routes. The road bears away to the right, rising to cross the railway and reach the main road just west of the railway station. At the main road you should turn left to reach the station. Alternatively, a well-blazed path goes straight ahead, through scrub, to emerge on the station platform, whence a footbridge leads over the railway to the car park and Conisbrough town. Despite its obvious use, this must be regarded as unofficial and cannot be recommended. Use the road instead.

Conisbrough and the Earth Centre

Conisbrough is well known for its 11th century castle, which featured in Sir Walter Scott's "Ivanhoe". It is arguably one of the finest Norman keeps in the country and well worth a visit if you have time. It is all too easy to dismiss Conisbrough as "just another mining town", but that would be unfair. The church dates back to the 7th century and is reputedly the oldest building in South Yorkshire. The village was an important royal manor at the time of the Norman Conquest. The pits that for so long stamped their mark on Conisbrough, are now both closed, Denaby in 1968 and Cadeby in 1986. Thus ended a 120 year old industry and with it went a way of life, thousands of jobs and associated industries. There remained a legacy of dereliction, which is only now beginning to vanish.

The biggest single project for regenerating the area is the Earth Centre. This multi million pound investment is designed to demonstrate the principles of "sustainable development". Over 300 acres of former colliery land is being used for the centre. The first phase, costing £2 million, comprises a refurbished railway station, a reception area and a link across the river to newly created gardens, woods and wetlands. Later phases involve the construction of a link to the castle, plus the building of a butterfly shaped structure housing various exhibitions. The Chief Executive of the project is Jonathan Swales, whose avowed intention is to create a centre which doesn't diminish or damage the earth's resources, instead "leaving the earth in as good a shape as we find it". An exciting and rewarding prospect.

7. Deepcar

The Route: Deepcar, Station Road, Wharncliffe Crags, Wharncliffe Lodge, Brownlow Rocher, Hallfield Head, Hall Wood, Low Spring, High Green, Low Hall Wood, Hazelshaw Farm, Smithy Fold, Hannah Moor, The Height, Station Road, Deepcar.

Distance: 12km (7.5 miles)

Start: Deepcar Station Road, for car drivers GR 291981. Public transport users should alight at the Royal Oak on Manchester Road.

Map(s): OS 1:25000 Pathfinder Series No. 726, Sheffield North and Stocksbridge

How to get there:

By public transport: There are daily services from Sheffield, Barnsley and Manchester.

By car: Follow the A616 Stocksbridge By-pass to its junction with the B6088. Follow the signs to Deepcar. Pass under the railway bridge and after 200 metres turn left along Station Road. Park neatly at the roadside before you get to the Don bridge.

The Walk

A convenient starting point is the Royal Oak on the main Manchester Road at Deepcar. From the pub, cross the main road and walk down the B6088. Cross the bridge over the Little Don and then turn right along Station Road. Go past the Lowood Working Men's Club on the left and then cross the bridge over the River Don. Just over the bridge there is a footpath sign on the left. Leave the lane here and go left, climbing steeply up through the trees. The path levels out, high above the river, by the pylons. In winter, Wharncliffe Crags can be seen on the right, through the trees. The view to the left is less attractive, consisting of the Stocksbridge Railway and the By-pass. The path soon joins a wider track, which trails in from the right. Straight on here, following the track which soon dips down to pass underneath the Stocksbridge Railway. Beyond the railway the track runs through more trees, still climbing, until it reaches another bridge. This carried the former Manchester to Sheffield electric railway over the path. In best tradition, having electrified the line by 1954, it was decided to concentrate all the Sheffield Manchester traffic on the Hope valley line instead, so the passenger service ceased in 1970 and the line closed entirely in 1980. What a waste.

Continue up the track through the trees, passing a small pond on the right. Streams run to the right and left of the track, which soon swings left to cross one of the brooks. Go straight on here, along a narrow path, which is waymarked, up through the trees.

Soon you reach a track which cuts across at right angles. Straight on across the track, following the waymarked path upwards. The path steepens markedly, almost becoming a scramble until suddenly it levels out at a small dam.

Keep to the right of the dam and soon pick up a narrow path which winds its way up through the trees, before bearing to the right and passing a pylon. Now you begin to rise above the trees. The path twists its way upwards, with glimpses to the north to Emley Moor television mast and Wortley village. Soon, still climbing, the path goes left, emerging abruptly on the edge of Wharncliffe Crags.

Along Wharncliffe Crags

The land falls away dramatically into the Don Valley. The view is tremendous, taking in the whole of Stocksbridge, with Underbank Reservoir beyond. A well-blazed path leads along the edge. It should be noted that most of the paths in this area are not rights of way, but they are permissive paths and some are waymarked. If in doubt consult the local highway authority.

This is a delightful walk, with superb views, often accompanied by the song of the skylark or the bubbling call of the curlew. It is hard to believe that you are so close to a major city and a large steelworks. Continue along the edge path to a fork. Keep left here and soon cross three streams in quick succession. Still on top of the crags, here called Upper Rocks, the path keeps close company with a stone wall. Over the wall you can see the woodland which surrounds The Height. Soon the path leaves the wall and bears right, through scrubby woodland. Another path joins from the right and here you bear left. The view is now to More Hall and Ewden Reservoirs,

Wharncliffe Crags

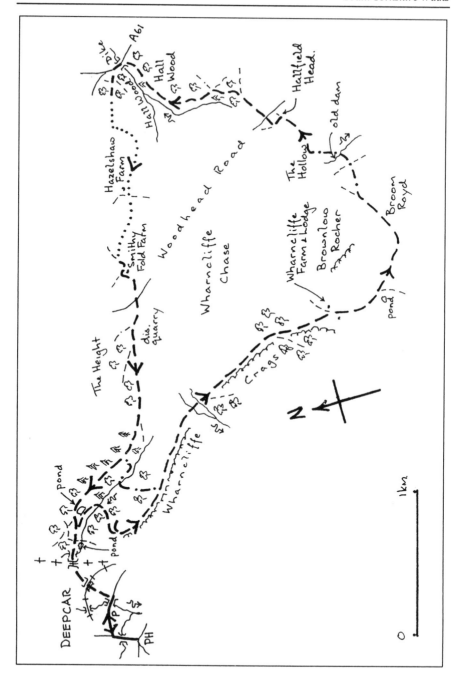

with the boats and wind surfers skimming across the surface like multi coloured insects.

Continue along through the clusters of rocks, though by now the dramatic edge of the crags has given way to more broken outcrops. At the fork in the path keep right. The view to the north and west takes in Emley Moor and Holme Moss masts, as well as the windmills near Penistone.

Wharncliffe Lodge

[Access to this section is only allowed on certain days; permission should be sought from Wharncliffe Estates, telephone 01142 882197]

Still keeping to the top of the edge, the path now reaches the isolated settlement comprising Wharncliffe Farm and Wharncliffe Lodge. The farm is to the left and the lodge, a rather fine old building, is to the right. Pass in front of the lodge and its attendant barns to a gate. The track continues through the gate and out onto open moorland again. To the left as you pass through the gate is the oddly named Brownlow Rocher. The "rocher" place name is not uncommon in this area. It comes from the Norman-French and means "rocks". The "low" element of Brownlow, presumably derives from the Norse "hlaw" and has a similar meaning to the many "low" place names found in the Peak District.

Follow the well-defined track across the moor, with good views ahead to Sheffield. See how many buildings you can identify at this distance; the University Arts Tower and the Hallamshire Hospital are obvious. At the Y-junction keep left, leaving the pond to the right.

Continue along the well-defined track which skirts round the foot of Browlow Rocher. As the track begins to head north east, towards the buildings which are identified on the map as The Hollow, there is a pair of stone gate posts. Just before these, the track forks again. Take the right-hand route here. It is not shown on the map at all, but it is distinct on the ground. Just past the shattered oak tree there is another fork in the path, again not shown on the map. Here go left along a narrow path across the moor. Ahead can be seen the boundary wall and in it can be discerned a stile and signpost. These lie well to the right of The Hollow. The path dips to cross a wet patch then crosses drier open moorland to the remains of a dam. This is shown on the OS map as a small square. Just beyond is the stile. Go over the stile, where you will find to your surprise that there is an almost illegible notice indicating that the moorland you have just left is private, but that it is open for public use on certain days. At least, that is what the author thinks it says, but the sign is so badly weathered that it is impossible to be certain. Questions to Barnsley Metropolitan Borough Council as to the status of paths on these moors indicate that they are permissive paths only, not rights of way. On this basis they can be closed at will. (See note at the beginning of this section).

Danger! Deep ruts

Walk past the trough, then go left, alongside the wall on a rough track. This at least is a public right of way. It also boasts some of the deepest ruts the author has ever seen. Don't fall in wet weather or you will certainly be drowned. At the end of the field the track enters a walled lane. The map shows the lane and the right of way going straight ahead to the farm. However, there is a waymarker which now directs you to the right, along a newly marked out route. This rejoins the lane to the right of the farm and the mapped route is then resumed, but not for long. The map shows a path bearing away to the left, diagonally across the field, heading for Hallfield Head. There is no sign of this path on the ground, no stile, gate or any indication that anyone has made any attempt to use the route. The author carried on up the track to Hallfield Head Farm, turning left just before the farm buildings. The track now slopes upwards to reach the farmyard gate. This has a Private notice fixed to it. Turn right here and go through the stile in the wall. A narrow path leads between a wall on the left and the barn on the right, to join a track. This soon disgorges onto the road.

Go straight across the road into another walled lane. The view from the top of this lane is very extensive, but it is soon lost as the lane develops into a deep hollow way. Soon the lane reaches the fringes of Hall Wood and forks. Go left here, ignoring the gate on the right and keeping just inside the wood. There is a view across to Potter Hill from here. The path delves deeper into Hall Wood, with a stream down below on the left. A well-defined path tends steadily downhill, eventually reaching a gate which takes you out onto the main Sheffield Barnsley road, the A61. There is no path on this side of the road so cross with care and go left along the footway

Forty winks

Mercifully, this sojourn along the A61 is brief. After about 200 metres you near the junction with the Huddersfield road, the A629. Look out for a footpath sign on the opposite side on the A61. Cross with care and go up the narrow, muddy path, which soon emerges into a wide open and even muddier area at the back of the farm. Make your way across the morass, ignoring the gate to the right, to reach a stile by another gate. This leads into a pleasant avenue of trees, through which there is sketchy path. At the end of the trees there is a stile in the fence ahead and a rather more distinct track going off to the left. Your route is over the stile, into the field and then alongside the wall on the left. This part of the walk was reconnoitred on a delightful Spring day and the author admits to taking forty winks in the meadow at this point, on the excuse of sitting down to admire the view.

Having woken up, continue alongside the wall, passing through a gateway or over the adjacent stile. The path now turns south west, but still follow the wall on your left, through another gateway. Here the path turns almost due west alongside the wall, to pass through this field to a gate and stile at the far end. Once through this stile, the path makes for Hazelshaw Farm. Keep the fence cum hedge on your right, thus avoiding the inquisitive bullocks. At the end of this field you will be confronted with a choice of a gate, a stile and then another gate to the right of the stile. The stile is the one you want. Do not go through the right-hand gate. This only leads into the farmyard.

On to Smithy Fold

Follow the hedge on the right to another stile at the far end of the field. Negotiate this stile and carry straight on, passing the barn to your right. The path now descends to reach a track and here you turn left. Almost at once there is a stile on the right taking you into open fields again. An indistinct path cuts through a series of fields before it rises to reach Smithy Fold. This array of buildings was in the throws of restoration when the walk was reconnoitred. The right of way passes along the front of the main buildings. Do not go through the gate at the end of the main buildings, but turn left and skirt the farmhouse, passing between it and a barn on the right. A short distance further on the track forks again. Here bear right and ascend the rough lane to reach the Woodhead Road.

At the road go right, but after less than 100 metres bear left along the signposted bridleway. This passes through a delightful stretch of woodland, full of the scent of bluebells in Spring. At the end of the wood there is a derelict and very overgrown quarry on the left. A waymark indicates a route bearing right but this is not your way. Instead, keep alongside the wall on the left, noting the small lake away to the right. A gateway soon leads you into an oak woodland. If you are tall enough to see over the wall there is a good view towards Stocksbridge and Ewden.

A natural divan

Just inside the wood the track forks again, and again there is a waymarker. Again you keep left, following the edge of the wood. This wood is a lovely mixture of different types of oak, birch, beech and sweet chestnut trees. Underneath the trees are soft tussocks of grass, "a natural divan and a good courting wood", as one of the author's companions remarked.

Follow the path as it descends by the wall, until a gateway is reached. The OS shows no junction of paths here, but there is one nevertheless. Carry on along the more obvious, right-hand route, ignoring the gateway to the left. The route is marked by small concrete posts with square tops, but this is purely fortuitous, for these are nothing to do with the path at all, but refer to a water main. The wood is now even more mixed, with various conifers and yew trees. After about 400 metres from the gate, the track bears right.

Carry on down the track, with trees on either side until you notice the small lake on the left-hand side amongst the trees. This is the second one you passed on your outward route. A track now leads off to the left. Follow this until you reach the point where your outward route crossed. It is waymarked, but could be missed. Turn right here, down the narrow path through the trees, following your outward route back under the two railway bridges. Beyond the second bridge keep a sharp look out for the path which leads off to the right, away from the track. It is waymarked, but the track is more obvious. Descend the steep bank with care, down to Station Road and retrace your steps either to your car or to the Royal Oak.

8. Doncaster

The Route: Kirk Sandall station, Grove Farm, Canal towpath, Long Sandall Lock, Canal "towpath", Doncaster Lock, North Bridge, Doncaster station.

Distance: 8.25km (5.1 miles)

Start: Kirk Sandall station GR 614078

Map(s): OS 1:25000 Pathfinder Series Nos. 717 Doncaster East and 716, Doncaster and Dearne.

How to get there:

By public transport: There is a frequent daily train service to Kirk Sandall from Doncaster on the Hull and Grimsby line.

By car: If you insist on using a car to access this walk, you should park in Doncaster, somewhere near the station and catch the train to Kirk Sandall from there. One way or another you will have to use the train at some point.

The Walk

[Access to the towpath is at the discretion of the British Waterways Board]

A moveable station

Catch the train from Doncaster to Kirk Sandall and alight there. If you are using the latest version of Pathfinder sheet 717 you will look in vain for Kirk Sandall station. If you are using the older 2½" to the mile sheet you'll be even more confused, because the station has moved! In the latter case, rely on the author's instructions, not the map.

From the station, go up the ramp and turn right, to cross the railway bridge. Cross the road just beyond the bridge and go left at the junction, using the short-cut path thoughtfully provided. Almost at once you reach The Glassmaker pub on your right; there is no other source of sustenance until you reach Doncaster.

Kirk Sandall

The church from which this village derives its name, is dedicated to St Oswald. He was instrumental in converting Northumbria back to Christianity after the disastrous Battle of Hatfield in 633 AD. The present church still has elements of the Norman building and is well worth a visit. It is particularly noted for its oak screen. The newer part of the village was laid out in the early part of this century in the well-known garden village style, by Pilkingtons when they built their new glass works nearby. Hence the name of the pub.

From the pub, continue along the main road, passing over the railway once more. On the left is an oddly wild area of scrub and gorse, strangely out of place in this otherwise urban setting. A short distance further on, go left at the junction and leave the main road behind. The little lane down which you now walk is far removed from suburbia. It is fringed with ditches and trees and you could be miles from anywhere, were it not for the glimpses of factory buildings on the left and of Thorpe Marsh power station ahead. On the right there is an obviously man made bank, but attempts to scale it and examine what was on top were defeated. Pity really, because this was the only serious ascent on the entire walk. The area east of Doncaster is not recommended for people training for mountaineering expeditions.

Onto the Navigation

The lane soon bends to the left and reaches Grove Farm. The older buildings of this farm are made from limestone, and look somewhat out of place, but they are a reminder that until fairly recently this stone would have been the indigenous building material. The lane skirts the farm and then goes left again, passing in front of the lovely little canalside chapel. Just by the chapel you reach a T-junction and here go right, to reach a fishermen's car park. Go through the car park to gain the canal bank and then turn left.

Chapel by the South Yorks Navigation at Kirk Sandall

For those used to the narrow canals of the Midlands, the Don Navigation comes as a shock. By British standards it is huge and deep. When the walk was reconnoitred however, there was a noticeable dearth of boats. We saw only one vessel moving and that was a cabin cruiser.

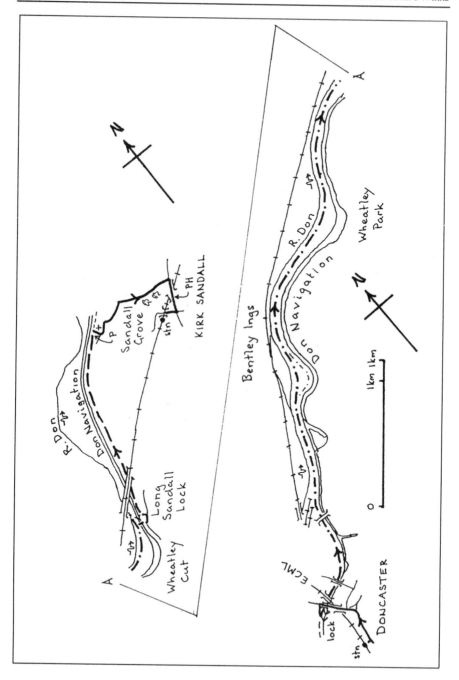

Follow the towpath, which is well-walked and muddy in places. It also bears ample evidence of that other common canalside pass time, fishing. Judging by the numbered posts there must be times when it is exceedingly difficult to walk along this path. It is worth bearing in mind that canal towpaths are not always public rights of way. Often they are concession paths and can be closed at will by British Waterways. This is the case with this section of path, so if you are in any doubt you should seek permission from the local British Waterways office.

After a short trot, or slide along the towpath, you pass under a high bridge which links two parts of a works. We were surprised to see line upon·line of new cars parked on the left, suitably defended by high fencing. The buildings now retreat from the canal side and the next obvious objective is the railway bridge. This marches defiantly across the navigation at a considerable skew. It is of course the line carrying the Doncaster to Kirk Sandall trains which you used a short time ago. Just beyond the bridge there are signs of activity on the canal, moored boats and buildings marking the approach to Long Sandall Lock.

Long Sandall Lock. Which way now?

The obvious continuation of the towpath leads through a gate, to the lock. The gate is clearly not intended to be used by mere walkers as it has a "PRIVATE, Keep Out" sign on it. A well-beaten path goes left, through the field to join a road. Here turn right and walk along the road, passing the lock buildings on the right and a derelict house on the left. Just beyond the lock buildings there is a car park for fishermen and boaters. The route is not obvious at this point. When we reconnoitred the walk we erroneously assumed that we should continue along the road. This is wrong, for the road soon swings away from the canal and there is no continuation of the towpath on this southern side. The trouble is that there doesn't seem to be any route on the northern side either.

Go through the car park and so regain the canalside. Cross the canal at the lock gates and then go over the bywash weir on the bridge. There is a stile in the fence ahead, just by a gate. The British Waterways workmen who were busily repairing the fence and cutting the grass by the lock confirmed that this was the route to Doncaster. "Over the stile and turn left. Follow the flood bank and you can't go wrong".

Go over the stile and onto the top of the flood bank. Here is the next shock, for there before you is the River Don. Its mud lined banks indicate that it is still tidal at this point, but what is more amazing is how close it is to the canal. Most of the remainder of this walk will lie along this thin strip of land between the two waterways.

The importance of weather forecasting

Some time after this walk had been checked, there was an announcement on the BBC national news that the train service between Doncaster and Hull had been suspended because of the Don flooding at Kirk Sandall. Not only should you check with British

Waterways, it would be wise to check with the weathermen too. There's not much high land to retreat to in case of a sudden flood.

A well-blazed path runs along the top of the flood bank and is easier than the lower tracks which have mainly been made by cattle. On the left is a fence which cuts you off from the canal. Ahead can be seen the spire of Bentley church. Soon the fence on the left ends and the river and canal move even closer together. Stick to the top of the bank, marvelling at the remains of a boat's rudder which grace the bank side and wondering what sort of a flood wrought such destruction.

St George's and the slave units

Continue ahead, not that you have much choice. Now the mighty tower of Doncaster's St George's church comes into view, usually with the saint's flag flying from the top. Despite the obvious Gothic nature of this church, it is actually a 19th century construction. The previous church was burned to the ground in a catastrophic fire. Well worth a visit if you have the time, if only to hear the organ, which is one of the finest in Britain. To the right can be seen the headgear of Bentley colliery and the stone spire of Arksey church. The land to the right is very low lying and the "ing" place names on the map indicate that flooding was once a regular occurrence. The Doncaster to Hull railway closely parallels the river and canal and there is a steady procession of passenger trains.

The factory on the far side of the canal proclaims that it makes "slave units". In this enlightened age, one wonders what these are and for which market they are intended.

The path keeps to the flood bank, rarely venturing near the canal. As a towpath this would have been useless. One wonders where the true towpath was. There must have been one, but it is certainly not obvious now. It was at this point we saw the one moving boat. Judging by the pronounced kink in the wake, the boatman was as surprised to see walkers as we were to see him, but we exchanged cheery waves nevertheless.

Not that there is an absence of boats at this point. There are plenty moored near Strawberry Island, but none showed signs of life. Presumably they must move at some time.

Smelly flows the Don

The strip of land between the canal and river is even narrower from now on and suddenly there is a hiatus. Across the path is a fence, with a gate, which plainly shows no desire to open. What is obvious however, is that many others have passed this way before, as there is a pronounced track on either side of the obstacle and in any case, this must have been the towpath route. This particular stretch is not too pleasant. There is a strange smell in the air that is difficult to define, except that it isn't nice. The river comes down a weir on the right and the canal veers away from the Don. The path loses sight of both river and canal as it thrusts through an area of scrub. Emerging from the scrub intrepid walkers will be amazed to find themselves confronted with two sets of railway buffer stops. The lines are still in place, but obviously disused. The path skirts to the left of the buffers and plunges back into scrub again, before descending to the canal side.

Now the walk becomes wholly urban. However, like so many urban canals, this one brings a swathe of greenery into the heart of the town. The towpath dips under a derelict railway bridge, which once served a factory on the south side of the canal. The main British Waterways wharf for Doncaster is now in view on the far side of the canal and an arm of the canal goes off to serve other wharves. At this point the 1:25000 map shows a proposed new bridge, "due to open 1994", but it hasn't. Recent pronouncements from the Department of Transport cast doubt on whether it ever will be built. Do readers know of any other examples of routes being included on a map and then not being constructed?

A road bridge spans the canal. This was under repair when the walk was being checked and the path was diverted round to the right, over the road and back down a flight of steps on the other side. In normal circumstances you will be able to walk under the road.

Under and over North Bridge

The end of the walk is now near. Marching across the canal at what seems a very low level, comes the East Coast Main Line railway, now electrified. Hidden underneath this massive bridge and the accompanying North Road bridge, is Doncaster Lock. It is so dark under the bridge that the lock seems to be in a tunnel and must be quite difficult to work. Pass under the bridges and past the lock keeper's office. A flight of steps and a ramp lead up to the right, onto the road, to give a dramatic return to the hustle and bustle of modern traffic. Turn right at the road and walk along the footway, down to the roundabout. There turn right to reach the railway station.

9. Dunford Bridge

The Route: Winscar Reservoir Picnic Site, Dunford Bridge, Trans-Pennine Trail, Cote Bank Bridge, Swinden Cottages, Far Swinden, Swinden Lane, Hordron Road, Hordron Bank, Loftshaw Clough, Fiddlers Green, Woodland Clough, Windleden Reservoir, Windleden Lane, Winscar Picnic Site.

Distance: 13km (8.1 miles)

Start: Winscar Reservoir Picnic Site, off Windleden Lane. GR 152018

Map(s): OS 1:25000 Outdoor Leisure Series No. 1 Dark Peak.

How to get there:

By public transport: daily services from Barnsley and Holmfirth to Dunford Bridge.

By car: A628 Trunk Road from east or west to its junction with Windleden Lane near Salters' Brook Bridge. Turn down Windleden Lane. The car park and picnic site is on the left after about 1.5 km (1 mile). From Holmfirth follow the B6106 to the junction signed to Dunford Bridge and Carlecotes. Turn right and follow the road through Carlecotes and Townhead to Dunford Bridge. The car park is beyond the village on the right.

The Walk

Wind Scour and windmills

From the Winscar Picnic Site, make your way back to Windleden Lane and turn left. The derivation of the name Winscar is obscure, but having reconnoitred this walk in January, the author and his companions are of the belief that it is a corruption of Wind Scour. Follow the road down towards the village, noting in the distance the 13 windmills of the new power station. They look quite impressive.

Dunford Bridge and its tunnels

There is no doubt as to the derivation of the name Dunford Bridge, but it indicates a very long history. The Dun element is Celtic meaning "water". Now of course it is the name of the river itself. The remaining two elements trace the different means of crossing the river at this point. The Stanhope Arms lies on the right, just before the bridge from which the village derives its name. To the left looms the grassed dam of Winscar reservoir, from which a white staircase of water cascades after heavy rain. The road passes over the remains of the Woodhead railway. The first cutting you pass is the "new" line, leading to the 1954 tunnel. Despite much effort this line was closed in 1980. The second cutting is the old line, leading to the 1845 and 1854 tunnels. The building of these lead to great loss of life and the conditions of the workers were the subject of a number of pretty damming reports. Paradoxically, considering that the old tunnels were closed to railway traffic in 1954, they are still in active use, carrying the main Trans Pennine power lines through the hill and, in order to service the cables, there is a narrow gauge railway through the tunnels as well. The tunnel mouths can all be seen from the bridge.

Along the Galway to Istanbul Trail

In October 1995, work is due to start on the conversion of the old railway into the TransPennine Trail, as part of the European route between Galway and Istanbul! However, the advised route at present is as follows:-

Continue up along the road (no footway) through the hamlet of Dunford Bridge. Ignore the road leading left towards Holmfirth and carry on until Townhead is reached, about 1 km (⅔ mile) from the railway bridge. Go past Upper Townhead Farm on the right and continue along the lane until it bends to the left. Here you should spot a faded footpath sign on the right, above a more obvious advert for "Western Riding". Go down the rough track which shows ample evidence of horse use, passing the farm on the right. The track now forks three ways. Yours is the middle one which has a signpost (sometimes) to Carlecotes. The track enters fields and bears right, and a series of stiles lead across a number of fields, making for the white house. At the white house a track is joined, which bears away left up the hillside, giving extensive views over the moors to the south.

Soon the road is reached and followed into Carlecotes. A sign on the right, points down a track. A glance at the map will show that this is not the OS version of the right of way, but it is correct never the less. Follow the track between the buildings until a msall gate is reached, with the words "To St Anne's Church" on it. Go through the gate and onto a narrow path which shoots round to the right of the church.

Beyond the church the path runs alongside the wall and woods of Carlecotes Hall. At the end of the wall there is a stile which takes you into a rough lane. Bear left here, still alongside the trees until the lane swings right at a gate. A stile by the gate takes you into fields and the track continues alongside a triangular clump of trees not shown on the map.

At the end of these trees the track continues ahead, but the path bears left across the field to reach a stile in the far wall, just to the left of the more obvious gate.

A sketchy path then leads across the next field to the rought lane at Soughley and thence over the infant Don to Cote Bank Bridge over the former railway.

Over Reddishaw Knoll

Go over the bridge, which is a concrete rebuild of 1950s vintage. At the far side, the track forks. Go left here along the waymarked path, until you reach a metal gate. At this point there is also a smaller wooden gate in the fence on your right and this is your route. It is waymarked as a bridleway. The path follows a wall on the left over a virtually flat area of rough grassland, not quite moor, not quite pasture. This is Reddishaw Knoll. Between the path and the grass is a deep ditch, which at the time this walk was checked, was full to overflowing. The walk then turned into an interesting exercise of tussock jumping. At one point, the farmer has positioned a

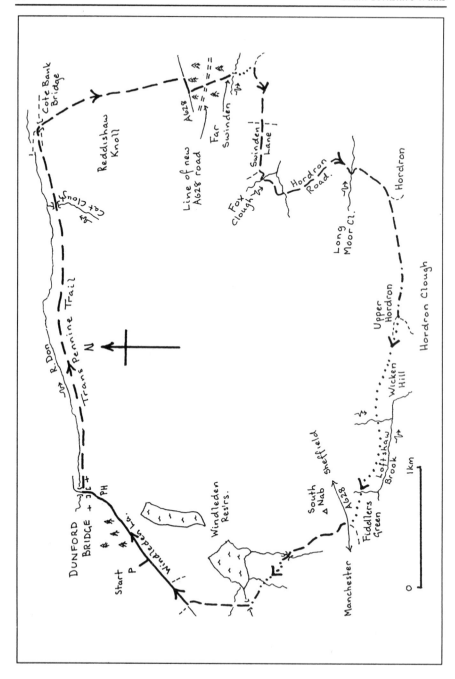

hefty plank bridge across the ditch. It was totally surrounded by water and looked for all the world like a raft.

From the relative safety of the raft you can afford to gaze around. The view is extensive but not spectacular, the landform is too flat for that. Eventually after much cursing and splashing, the end of the field was reached and a gate lead into a marginally drier, walled lane. This parallels Reddishaw Knoll Plantation and emerges onto the main A628 between Acre Head Cottage and White Cottage. Dog owners should note that Acre Head Cottage is home to a large Alsatian, but his bark is worse than his bite, (so we were told). (If you feel in need of refreshment, or the bus back to Barnsley, both can be found by turning left at this point and making your way along the A628 for 400-500 metres to The Flouch Inn).

On to Swinden Farm

The A628 is a very fast and very busy road, but this section will be superseded in the very near future, as a new road is being built through the plantation further south. Turn right at the cottages and go along the A628 for about 150 metres, then cross, with care, to the signed path through the trees. The first part of the path was very wet and squelchy when checked, but it improved markedly thereafter. The trees are all conifers, but you can at least look along the forest ride and see the open hillside of Hingcliff Common rising ahead. The new road will cross near this point and is now under construction. The track begins to descend and then does a sharp left-hand turn by the ruins of Far Swinden Farm. Do not go left here, but carry straight on, passing the ruins and then bearing right between the buildings and the trees, to reach a stile.

Go over the first stile, ignore the superfluous second stile and negotiate Kiln Bank Brook to reach open fields, where all semblance of a path vanishes. Go straight across the field until the far wall comes into view and with it a gate, marked by a signpost. Go through the gate, or over the adjacent stile, and turn right along Swinden Lane. The lane is as marked on the map, a track, and is the access to Swinden Farm.

The Swinden Lane Motorway

The walled track rises steadily and easily, to a fork. The obvious route is straight on, but this is private. The less obvious route lies to the right. This is the right of way and it is signed with a finger post and a large Keep Right sign, which has mysteriously migrated here from some busier road. Go right and continue along the walled track.

MI6, spies or nuns?

Soon you come to a crossing of tracks, but carry straight on. The route to the left leads to a rather fine looking house, very isolated and not named on the 1:25000 map. Speculation as to its use ranged from "a safe house for MI6" to "a nunnery". The larger scale maps record the place as Swinden Lodge, which gives a clue as to its purpose in this out of the way spot.

Leaving the lodge behind, carry on along Swinden Lane, until you reach a gate by an Access to Open Country sign. Go over the stile alongside the gate and bear left, leaving Swinden Lane in favour of Hordron Road. The use of the word "road" for this track is an even bigger misnomer than the previous use of "lane" in Swinden

Lane. Hordron Road consists of two ruts, which zigzag down to a ford across Fox Clough Brook, one of the tributaries of the Little Don. The ford is usually no trouble, but after heavy rain crossing can be a problem. You either have to negotiate the barbed wire infested railings which span the stream, just above a little waterfall, or you will have to make your way up stream and jump. There is no bridge and the ground on the far bank is invariably wet.

Hordron Road then climbs away from the stream, beside a wall. It is tempting to venture through one of the many gaps to sit on the bank overlooking the stream and the pleasantly wooded Fox Clough, but beware, for the wall is unstable and can collapse at the slightest touch.

A fine view

Still climbing, the track swings away from the clough. The higher you climb, the better the view to the south and east. Margery Hill can be seen to the south, at 546 metres, one of the highest places in South Yorkshire. Eastwards there is a view down the valley of the Little Don towards Langsett. The track now turns south and runs across a wide expanse of moorland which the map names as Barmings. Again the views south and east are extensive, though there is little to see to the west as the land rises gently in this direction and cuts off any long distance view. Northwards you can see the television mast at Emley Moor. Two small streams are crossed without difficulty, even in very wet weather. These are Great Grain and Little Grain.

Still with a wall to the left, the "road" now dips down towards Long Moor Clough Brook. A few wind blasted pines seem to indicate that at one time there may have been a plantation here, but the trees have nearly given up the unequal struggle. In the bottom of Long Moor Clough, the map again indicates a ford. Like its predecessor, this ford has no footbridge and requires long jump skills in wet weather. Beyond the brook the track rises again, leaving the confines of the clough and passing out onto Little Moor. The track is no longer enclosed by a wall as it swings south west and begins to head up the main valley of the Little Don.

At the top of the hill the track turns west and here there is a standing stone. At some time it has been used as a gatepost, but it may be the remains of a guidestone or wayside cross. Just past the stone the track forks, the left-hand route going through a gate in a fence and descending to Hordron. The right-hand route is the one you want and this runs alongside the fence and wall for a further 800 metres until Upper Hordron is reached. The track then passes through a gateway to reach the building.

Upper Hordron, any port in a storm

If shelter is required, Upper Hordron provides it. It was obviously a substantial barn at one time, but it has been rebuilt with a lean to type of roof. The barn has three "rooms". Two are securely locked bolted and barred, with heavy metal doors. These are for shooting parties. The third room is open and this is for sheep, but walkers could use it in cases of dire need. The new dividing walls between the rooms are of genuine Tarmac Topblock, or so the author was told by one of his companions who is knowledgeable about these matters.

There is actually no need to visit the barn of Upper Hordron at all, for a narrow, indistinct path continues alongside the boundary wall, keeping to the same alignment as the previous "road". If you have gone to the barn, a good track skirts round the back of the building, emerging into a field. The track forks in mid field, one branch descending as shown on the map, into the confines of the clough. The other, not shown on the map, bears right, passing through a gap in the field wall, to emerge on the open hillside. Follow this right-hand path.

Feel the Earth move for you

When the reconnoitre of this walk was undertaken there were two places on this piece of path where the earth literally moved beneath our feet. Presumably the peat below the grass was completely waterlogged and liquid. Fortunately the grass held firm, but it was an interesting feeling. The track soon rejoins the route which skirted Upper Hordron and continues for a short way before ending at a patch of bare earth.

A barely discernible path, little more than a sheep track, continues across the flat area between Hordron Bank on the left and Long Moor Edge on the right. Straight ahead is the curious Laund Clough, which has two streams in it. Both can be seen from this vantage point. There is only a narrow strip of higher land between the two.

The Traverse of Loftshaw Clough

Your path swings north west into Loftshaw Clough, still keeping well up the hillside and not dropping down the steep slope to the water's edge. On the right, up the hill, can be seen a line of shooting butts. Continue below these, sometimes losing the path, which by now is definitely no more than a sheep track.

Still continuing on a north westerly course, note on the left and below, the sharp features of Wicken Hill. The western flank of this curious knoll plunges very steeply into Loftshaw Clough. Continue to contour the hillside, still heading north west. You will now be looking straight up Lofshaw Clough. A subsidiary clough opens up on the right, quite a deep cleft, heading almost due north. As you approach this clough, you will notice a fence on the horizon to your right. Despite the apparent wildness of this area, the fence tells you that you are only 500 metres away from the busiest trunk road in the National Park. If you are fed up with moorland and fancy the hustle and bustle of the trunk road, it is an easy step up the stream.

For the purists however, the site of the fence is an anathema. You will therefore hurry into the cleft of the clough on the sheep track kindly provided, cross the stream with all speed and scramble up the other side onto the flanks of Loftshaw Clough. There is no path here at all, so make your way with care amongst the tussocks, bracken and heather, losing no height, but heading west now, up the main valley of Loftshaw Clough. This area is shown on the 1:25000 map as Loftshaw Holes.

About 500 metres from the last stream crossing, you come to another, smaller, but more boggy trickle, complete with its own little clough. Cross this where the sheep have been before and beaten down a passage through the rushes. Once on the other side, begin to bear away from the main valley, up the hillside to the right. If your navigation and the author's description is anything like accurate, you will soon top the rise and the A628 should be before you. This is Fiddlers Green, though how it got that name is a mystery.

Fiddlers' Green and the old Coach Road

The road is fenced from the moor, but you should have emerged near to the gate and stile which marks the point where the old coach road leaves the modern highway. If you have crested the rise just to the east of the gate, you would be well-advised to follow the top of the ridge, such as it is, until you reach the old road and then use that to reach the gate. The ground between the ridge-top and the A628 is very wet and boggy, except where the old road crosses. There is a good view over to Black Hill from here, with the television mast at Holme Moss clearly in view.

Immediately opposite the point where you emerge onto the A628, there is a bridleway sign and this is your route. Cross the A628 with care and follow the bridleway across a very wet patch, until you gain the relatively dry western slope of South Nab. The trig point is just to your right.

Down to Windleden

The bridleway soon begins to descend quite rapidly and the reservoirs at Winscar and Windleden come into view. There is no difficulty in following the path, which is well-defined as it drops steadily into the southern end of Woodland Clough. However, this is deceptive. The track crosses the Woodland Clough Brook on a very nice dry stone culvert and continues plainly ahead towards a gateway. However, just over the bridge and before the gateway, there is a post on the left-hand side, part way up the bank. This is a waymarker for the bridleway, which bears left at this point, leaving the obvious track. There is only scanty evidence of use of the waymarked route, until a bridle gate is reached in the wall overlooking Broad Clough. The route then drops steeply down the hillside, heading for the left-hand tip of the reservoir. It is likely that this route was a diversion when the reservoir was built, as it is not an obvious bridleway and shows no signs of being used as such, being far too steep.

At the bottom of the hill, the path crosses Broad Clough Brook on a solid plank bridge. it then swings to the west, round the shoulder of the hill, separated from the reservoir by a classic water board metal fence. At the corner of the fence the path drops to the inlet stream, which again sports a substantial plank bridge. The stream looked deceptively shallow, but our canine companion soon discovered that it was not so.

Beyond the stream the path bears away to the right, slanting up the hillside, with a view over both Windleden reservoirs. Soon the Windleden Lane comes into view ahead and the tower marking the air shaft onto the Woodhead tunnel. Turn right at the road and complete the walk by an easy descent to Winscar Picnic Site.

10. Eastfield

The Route: Eastfield (Bagger Wood), Lower Lea Wood, Eastfield, Tom Royd Wood, Berry Moor House, Dodworth Moor End, Silkstone Trail, Lower Fallthwaite, Bagger Wood Dike, Bagger Wood.

Distance: 6km (3.7 miles)

Start: Bagger Wood car park GR303024 (if you can find it!)

Map(s): OS 1:25000 Pathfinder Series No. 715 Barnsley and Penistone

How to get there:

By public transport: There is a Monday to Saturday service from Barnsley to Eastfield.

By car: This is one of those annoying places that ought to be easy to find, but aren't. From Barnsley it is probably easiest to follow the B6099 over the M1 before turning left and following the signs to Stainborough and Hood Green. Beyond Hood Green you are on Bagger Wood Road and the wood itself soon appears on the right. There is a sign indicating a picnic site ahead, but that is the last indication you'll get. There is no picnic site and the car park is unsigned but almost opposite Bagger Wood Farm. If you reach the Eastfield pub, you've gone too far. From the west, turn off the A629 at Thurgoland, following the signs for Silkstone. Less than a kilometre out of Thurgoland you pick up the signs for Stainborough and Hood Green. Follow these and you should soon pass the Eastfield pub. The (unsigned) car park is about 400 metres beyond the pub, on the left, almost opposite Bagger Wood Farm.

The Walk

Escape from the Hidden Car Park

From the car park, if you find it, go up onto the road and turn right. There is no footway along the road so take care, cars do come at quite a speed along here. Ignore the footpath sign on the opposite side of the road and look carefully in the trees on the left to see if you can spot the picnic site which is marked on the map and indicated by the road signs.

Turn left and then, almost at once, left again at a signposted stile. The path is indistinct but crosses a small field to another stile. Here you are in a thin belt of trees, which mark the site of a former railway line that served a colliery at Crane Moor. Nature has completely reclaimed its own. Follow the waymarks across the line to another stile. Bear left in the next field to reach yet another stile, which takes you into Lower Lea Wood. This woodland and that at Bagger Wood, are in the ownership of the Woodland Trust. Within certain limits they allow open access to their property and are dedicated to the upkeep of the woodlands in a traditional manner. None of your serried ranks of conifers here. The Trust deserve your support and their efforts to keep these woodlands in pristine condition should be respected.

Eastfield. Again!

Inside the wood the path is more obvious and easy to follow. Soon the edge of the wood is reached and the path continues downwards, with the trees to the left and a fence and fields to the right. At the end of the wood another stile drops you neatly onto the bridge over the Bagger Wood Dike. Climb away from the stream, with the fence to your right, noting the pigeon lofts at Eastfield just ahead. This is the place shown on the map as Eastfield. A stile by the gate leads into a driveway and thus onto the road, where you should turn right. About 200 metres down the road there is a footpath sign on the left and a stile. From this point there is a good view over the upper reaches of the Dove Valley to Barnsley. Go through the stile and follow the hedge and wall until you reach the trees. A stile takes you into Tom Royd Wood and a distinct path follows the wall on the right-hand side. Soon the path forks. The right-hand route is shown on the OS map, but isn't a right of way, so that limits your choice. Bear left and follow the brick paved path down through the wood, keeping close to the left-hand edge of the trees for about 200 metres. The wood then widens out and the path descends through the trees to reach a crossing of routes, which isn't shown on the map. Go straight on here to reach a stile at the bottom of the wood.

Smile Sweetly at the Dogs

Once over the stile, cross the bridge which spans the small stream and then bear right, climbing up the field, towards the buildings. There is a stile by a gate at the left of the Nissen hut. Go through the stile onto the farm lane and pass the hut on the left, smiling sweetly at the dogs. Just past the hut and before the main farm buildings, a rough track goes off to the left. This is your route. Follow the rough lane up to Berry Moor House where there is a T-junction. Just before the junction there is a stile in the wall on the right. Go over this and follow the wall, now on your left, past the farm buildings until you locate another stile. Go through this and then bear diagonally right across the field. There is a stile in the far corner. Go right, by the fence, not through the gate, and follow the track alongside the wall cum hedge, through a couple a stiles. Nether Royd Wood Nature Reserve is to your left. Where the path leaves the guiding hedge, at a stile by a gate, bear left across the field. Keep to the left of the buildings of Dodworth Moor End and you will locate a stile by a hawthorn bush, midway between the first and second electricity pylons from the house. This stile deposits you on a track just above the junction with House Carr Lane. Walk down to the junction and there go right.

Silkstone

Silkstone lies just a short distance to the left. An old settlement, with a fine Norman church, Silkstone became economically important with the growth of the coal mining industry in the 19th century. The village gave its name to one of the coal seams and a huge piece of Silkstone coal was exhibited at the Great Exhibition of 1851. More

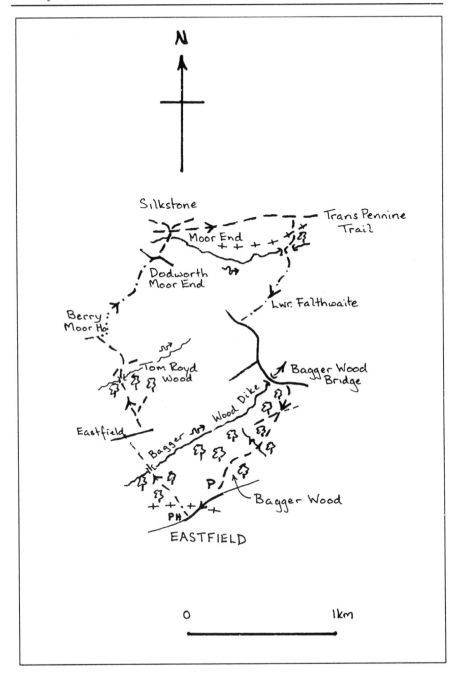

N

Silkstone

Trans Pennine
Trail

Moor End

Dodworth
Moor End

Berry
Moor Ho.

Lwr. Falthwaite

Tom Royd
Wood

Bagger Wood
Bridge

Eastfield

Bagger Wood Dike

Bagger Wood

P

PH

EASTFIELD

0   1km

tragically, but only too common in this industry, there is a memorial in the church-yard to 26 children, the youngest only 7, who were drowned in a pit disaster in 1838. Now the pits and their associated industries and transport infrastructure have all gone.

In less than 100 metres there is a footpath sign on the left and a stile. Go left here, leaving the road and re-entering fields. Bear right, across the field, descending towards the trees which fringe the brook. Keep to the left of the obvious dead tree and thus locate a bridge over the deep cleft of the Moor End Brook. Climb up from the brook, ignoring the temptation to try your hand at the rope swing kindly provided by the local youngsters, until you reach a bridge. This bridge used to carry the Wath to Penistone railway line, which was built solely for goods traffic and in particular, coal. By railway standards the line was steeply graded and trains were "banked" up the hill, with one or two locomotives at the front and another two pushing behind. About a kilometre to the west, the line goes through a notorious tunnel, where the conditions for the enginemen on the rear banking engines must have been sheer hell. The line was electrified in the early 1950s, but the coal trains still needed bankers. The cessation of coal deliveries from South Yorkshire pits to Fiddlers Ferry power station meant the end for this route. It has now been converted into a footpath, part of the Trans Pennine Trail.

Memories of a Mis-spent Youth

Do not go under the bridge, but instead go up the steps to the right and thus onto the railway embankment. This was a salutary experience for the author as the last time he had been at this spot was as a passenger on an excursion train in the mid 1960s. On gaining the embankment go right. The trail soon clears the trees and enters a cutting. Hard to believe that there was a double track railway on here less than 20 years ago.

Pass under the occupation bridge and soon, to your right you can see the remains of the former Moor End branch line, which served the long closed Moor End colliery. It is hard now to imagine that a coal mine ever existed, but you will see remnants of it later in the walk. About 400 metres beyond the bridge, look out for a stile on the left. Do not go over it, but now look right and there should be a stile in the opposite fence. When this walk was reconnoitred this stile was well-hidden by vegetation and was easily missed. The stile takes you off the railway and back into fields. Go straight across the field, to a gap in what was once a hedge, just to the right of a silver birch tree. You are now on the Moor End branch. Go straight across, noting that some kind soul has provided a wooden seat where the boundary fence would have been. Either that, or it is the remnant of a stile. The line and the embankment beyond are heavily overgrown, but the path is obvious enough. As you begin to descend the embank-ment, there are the remains of buildings to your right, hidden in the trees. The ruins include some massive stone structures, whose purpose can only be guessed at. No doubt some colliery historian will know exactly what these buildings were. The path skirts to the left of the ruins and drops quite steeply down the side of what seems to be an overgrown spoil heap. Soon the path turns right to run alongside the stream and emerge from the wood. At this point there is a footbridge on the left.

Lower Fallthwaite

Cross the stream and head up the field with the fence and hedge on your left. The hedge curves to the right and you continue to follow it, until you reach a gateway. Pass through the gateway, no stile, and carry straight on, heading towards the buildings of Lower Fallthwaite Farm. Keep to the right of the farm, alongside the wall and so reach another gateway, which is waymarked. There is a pond just to the left and when the author past this way he disturbed a heron. Carry on along the waymarked and tree lined track, passing the pond, and thus reach House Carr Lane again. Go left here, along the road. There is no footway but there is not much traffic either, so you should be safe enough. Just take care.

After a couple of hundred metres there is a bridleway sign on the left, but you should ignore this and continue along the road. Where the lane makes a bend to the left, there is a fine range of old buildings which form part of Fallthwaite Grange Farm. Some of the buildings are of half timbered construction. At the T-junction just beyond Fallthwaite Grange Farm, continue straight ahead, along Baggerwood Hill. Bagger Wood itself can now be seen ahead, just over the stream.

Thanks to the Woodland Trust

Pass the Hood Green sign and go over the bridge which spans the Bagger Wood Dike. The road now steepens appreciably as Bagger Wood is reached. Look out for the Woodland Trust sign on the right, for this marks an access into the woodland. Go into the wood and follow the narrow path, which makes its way steeply up, through the trees, until a broad track is reached. The initial, narrow path is not shown on the map, but the broad track is. Neither are rights of way, but the Trust welcomes caring visitors. At the track go right and enjoy a delightful woodland ramble. The track soon forks and you should bear left here, though both routes will eventually get you back to the car park. The track steadily ascends through the wood to reach a cross "roads". Straight on here, now descending sharply to cross a culverted stream. Beyond the stream the path rises again, passing a large water tank on the left. Very soon you reach a stile and the car park is just to the right.

This walk relies on the open access policies of the Woodland Trust for its very existence. Please respect their woodlands and if you care to make a donation to this worthy cause, the address is Autumn Park, Dysart Road, Grantham, Lincs. NG31 6LL. Check on one of their notice boards just to make sure.

11. Elsecar

The Route: Elsecar, Linthwaite, The Needle, Lee Wood, Hoober Stand, Street Lane, Cortworth House, Wentworth Woodhouse, Wentworth, Barrowfield Gate, Low Wood, King's Wood, Elsecar.

Distance: 9.25km (5.75 miles)

Start: Elsecar Car Park. GR. 385995

Map(s): OS 1:25000 Pathfinder Series No. 726 Sheffield (North) and No. 727 Rotherham.

How to get there:

By public transport: Daily bus services from Barnsley and Rotherham. Train services from Sheffield, Barnsley, Huddersfield and Leeds.

By car: Not the easiest place to find. From the M1 at Tankersley follow the A6135 to its junction with the B6097 at Hoyland Common. Turn left and keep on the B6097 through Hoyland to Elsecar. At the T-junction by the Market Inn, go right to reach the car park.

The Walk

How to avoid a tempting pub

Go from the Elsecar car park onto the main road and turn right. Walk past the Market Inn then go right, along the lane signed to Elsecar Heritage Centre. The heritage centre is just on the left down the lane and is well worth a visit. The car park for the centre is on the right and there is access through it from the main public car park which is the starting point of this walk. If you cannot bear to walk past the Market Inn, you can avoid the temptation by cutting through the heritage centre car park. For anyone interested in industrial archeology the Elsecar Heritage Trail is a must. Much of the village is a conservation area and it is well worthy of the designation. Much of the interest centres round the fact that the local landowners, the Earls Fitzwilliam, took such an enlightened attitude towards their businesses and workforce. Particularly noteworthy are the Miners Lodging House, the Earl's private station and the Newcomen beam engine. Take the time to browse round.

Continue up the lane, across the mill stream until the lane deteriorates to a rough track and forks. Go left here, following the sign post and proceed up through the scrub until you reach a patch of open ground. Keep right here, following the remnants of a field boundary. The heritage centre lies below you and to the left. The path soon shows signs of having been a lane at one time, as it has a hedge on either side. Ignore paths going off left and right and continue straight on up until you reach a signpost and a stile at a crossing of tracks. This is at the corner of Kings Wood. From here there is a good view back to Elsecar Church. Carry straight on here, across the field, making for the pylon on the horizon. At the next stile, bear right, heading now for the clump of trees, seen ahead. As the path rises steadily, there is a view to the right, over the trees of Kings Wood to the distant hills of the Pennines.

Bull Run

When we walked this route it was during a very dry spell and the ground was hard baked with huge cracks in the clayey soil. After rain it could be both muddy and slippery. Go through the next stile and follow the fence on your right to the clump of trees seen earlier. There was a bull in this field when the walk was reconnoitred and the author and his companion spent the time estimating how long it would take them to climb the fence and how long it would take the bull to reach us. Fortunately the bull was too hot and had other things on his mind to bother about chasing us, but he did stand perilously close to the stile at the top of the field.

At the stile go straight on, under the power line, with the fence and hedge right. Keppel's Column is in view to the right. It was built in 1778, to commemorate Admiral Keppel's acquittal of a charge of cowardice and not, as one might expect, to celebrate a naval victory. Ahead can be seen the tower blocks in the southern suburbs of Sheffield. Wentworth Church lies just to the right and beyond are the hills of the Peak District, blue in the haze. The pyramidal shape of Hoober Stand can be seen ahead and left. At the end of the field there is a gateway and stile on the right. Go through this and continue alongside the fence, though it is now on your left. This is very much a ridge-top path. Not spectacular like a mountain ridge, but giving commanding views both sides nevertheless. Pass through another stile whereupon there is the fence to the left and the remnants of a hedge to the right. A further stile soon follows and this takes you back to the other side of the fence as you approach Lee Wood.

At this point on the reconnoitre we were in deep discussion about which power station we could see to the north (left) and what the curiously shaped tower was for. We had managed to identify Wombwell and Wath and were so busy with these deliberations that we completely missed one of the highlights of the walk, the Needles Eye. Shamefacedly we had to retrace our steps to find it.

Through the Eye of the Needle

As you reach the edge of Lee Wood, ignore the view left and look for a gateway on the right. This leads through the hedge into an open area of the wood, in which stands the Needle. How we missed it I shall never know, for it is big enough to drive a coach and horses through the "Eye". Indeed the legend is that it was built for the purpose of winning a bet that a coach could be driven through the eye of a needle. The construction date is not known exactly, the information board explaining that it was built either in 1722 or 1780. It is one of a number of follies or feature buildings that form part of the Wentworth estate and which were designed to be seen from the mansion of Wentworth Woodhouse.

Return to the path and go right, keeping alongside the wood until you reach a kissing gate. This takes you onto the road. Cross the road and go down Street Lane

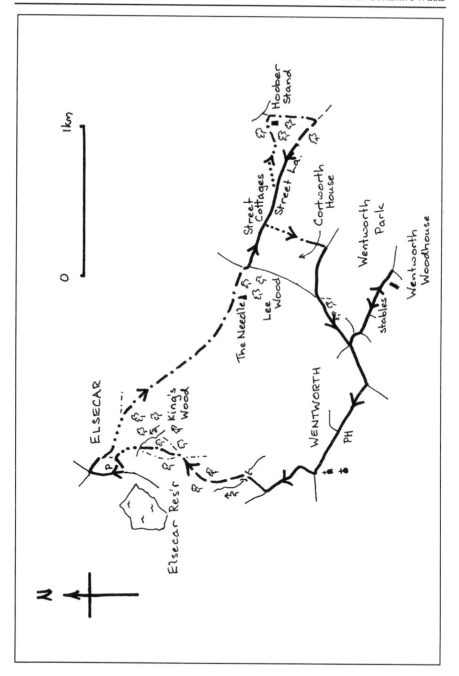

almost opposite. There is a seat here by the pillar box, just in case you are worn out. The place name Street is usually associated with the presence of a Roman road. The path you have just come on and its continuation as Street Lane have all the hallmarks of such a route. Follow this narrow metalled lane, past the cottages of Street hamlet, a lovely collection of buildings. About 200 metres beyond the last house, there is a path leading off to the left, marked by a footpath sign. The route goes to the right, diagonally across the field, making for Hoober Stand, which can now be seen in the midst of its fringing trees. There were cattle in this field at the time we tried out this walk and mindful of the earlier bull we kept a close watch on their movements. The path soon reaches the remains of a hedge on the far side of the field and then bears right, following the power line to reach a stile into the wood. Just inside the wood, the path forks. Bear left here and continue on the broad track which runs on a terrace through the trees. The Stand can be glimpsed through the trees to the right. Little paths veer off at intervals towards the Stand, but you are advised to continue along the track until you reach what appears to be someone's back garden. It is, but the path passes through it to reach a rough lane at a gate. Go right here and so reach Hoober Stand.

Hoober Stand

This is a most curious structure, triangular in plan and tapering towards the top. The funny little excrescence on the roof apparently covers the top of the stairs, but the effect is to make the building seem lop-sided and likely to fall over at any minute. Perhaps this is nearer the truth than might be supposed, for there is no access to the interior due to the danger of collapse following mining subsidence. However, there has obviously been extensive remedial work done on the tower, so hopefully it won't be long before you can again climb the stairs and admire the view from the top. The information board states that the tower was built between 1747-9 to commemorate the safe deliverance of England from the Jacobite rebellion. From the top of the 85ft tower you are supposed to be able to see York Minster.

Returning to the path, go right and descend the green lane. Rotherham is in view ahead and left, and Rawmarsh church stands out well. Continue down the green lane through a couple of stiles until you reach a track. This is Street Lane again, though here it is unmetalled. Go right at this point. Hoober Stand can occasionally be glimpsed through the trees on the right. A little further on, on the left there are brief visions of a little lake. You soon rejoin your outward route and by now the lane is metalled. At the cottages look out for a footpath sign on the left. A stile takes you over into fields. Stroll down the field with the hedge to your right. Ahead, in the parkland of Wentworth Woodhouse, you will spot a curious round barn. Further away to the left is the pillared structure which formed the Mausoleum.

At the bottom of the field, a gate leads out into the driveway of Cortworth House. Continue down the drive to another gate and thus reach the main road (B6090 for those with a passion for road numbers). Here turn right. There is a footway on this side of the road, so there is no need to cross. At the road junction, continue along the main road until you come to the Wentworth sign. On the opposite side of the road is the North Lodge, with no access now to Wentworth Woodhouse. If you turn your back on the lodge and the main road and look across the fields, you can clearly see The Needle, which you visited earlier. The various structures were designed to be viewed from a distance from the main park. You will see another example of this later.

Wentworth Woodhouse

Continue along the main road until the principal entrance to Wentworth Woodhouse Park is reached. It is not strictly necessary to visit the park on this walk, but it is well worth the deviation. Cross the road and go through the gateway. As soon as you emerge from the initial trees into the parkland proper, you can see Hoober Stand away to the left. You could also count yourself unlucky if you didn't see a few of the resident herd of red deer. Its a pity about the modern buildings on the left. Definitely not an enhancement to the scene. The driveway joins that from the North Lodge and soon reaches the imposing stable block. Note the bell tower and the sundials. The north west facing sundial face is particularly interesting. The driveway now skirts the walled garden of the mansion itself and then the whole south eastern aspect of this magnificent house comes into view.

The house was the country seat of the Earls Fitzwilliam and remained in the family until the death of the 10th earl in 1979. Fortunately he had taken the precaution of setting up a trust to administer the estate and maintain the village.

Wentworth Woodhouse

Retrace your steps past the stables to the main road. As you emerge, note on the opposite side of the road the Round House, another curious structure in an area famed for them. At the main road go left, not crossing the road this time.

Wentworth village

As you pass the workshops that have developed in the old estate buildings on the left, take care, for the large weigh-bridge is cracked and dangerous. At the road junction by the cross, go right and proceed along the main street, passing the post office and the first of Wentworth's pubs. Pass the public car park on the right, an unassuming place, unsigned but well-looked after. Then on the left is the delightful Paradise Square. Thus you come to the George and Dragon, and unless you are very late or very strong willed you will undoubtedly turn aside here to sample its delights. Note the bus stop just outside the pub, just in case!

Leaving the George and Dragon, turn left and continue along the main street. Wentworth is a lovely estate village, still largely unspoiled and retaining some interesting remnants of estate based industries. As you reach the end of the main street, look left to the "new" church, a large commodious building built in 1877. The old church is still there too, and you will see this a few yards further on. This dates back to the mid 13th century and contains the mortal remains of one of Wentworth's most famous sons, Thos. Wentworth, Earl of Strafford. His loyalty to his king, Charles I, led to his execution in 1641. At the end of the main street, where the road forks, go right, and descend Barrowfield Lane.

Back to Elsecar

As you go along the lane you will see to the left the old windmill. Ignore the footpath sign on the right, where the road bends to the left. Continue along the road instead for about another 300 metres. You soon reach the access for the Wentworth Sawmills, a concrete road, which also boasts a footpath sign. Go right here, passing the sawmills and follow the narrowing concrete strip as it dips to cross a stream, then rises through an area of scrubby woodland, to reach a gateway. There is a view back from this point, to Wentworth village, with the church being particularly prominent. At the fork in the track, just inside Kings Wood, bear right and follow the path through the oak woods until you reach another junction. Here bear left and descend through the wood to reach a gap in the boundary. A path joins from the left and together they proceed into the field. There is no obvious path across the field, but head to the left of the metal pylon. The car park is now in view ahead. A gap in the wall ahead drops you into a narrow track. Turn left here and walk down to the road, then turn right, to reach the car park.

12. Fishlake

The Route: Fishlake, Great Ing, Don Bank, Town Ing, Hangmans Hill Bridge, Thorninghurst Fm, Clough House Farm, Sour Lane, Fishlake.

Distance: 6.5km (4 miles)

Start: Roadside parking near Fishlake Post Office. GR 655132

Map(s): OS 1:25000 Pathfinder Series No. 705, Thorne

How to get there:

By public transport: amazingly, there's a daily service to Doncaster!

By car: M18 to Junction 6, (the A614). Follow the A614 towards Goole and at Hangmans Hill, about 1km from the M18 go left over the girder bridge. Follow this road into Fishlake, turning left on the road signed to Stainforth. Continue on the Stainforth Road until you reach the Post Office on the left.

The Walk

Fishlake village

The walk begins from the Post Office in the middle of Fishlake. Alongside the Post Office is a pleasant village green with an information board. This gives details of the Fishlake Historical Trail, which, combined with this walk would give a good day's exploration of the area. Despite the obvious modern meaning of the place name, the true meaning is slightly different. The place-name "Fiscelac" first appears in Domesday in 1086 and derives from the Old English meaning a fish stream, not a lake. From the Post Office head along the road towards the Hare and Hounds and the church. The pub is fascinating, but so is the church. It has what is thought to be the oldest Norman doorway in the country and is dedicated to St Cuthbert, the fabled saint from Holy Island in Northumberland. Legend has it that when the Danes began their invasions, the monks from Holy Island carried the body of Cuthbert away to safety. At each place where the body lay, a cross was erected, and in some cases a church. Such is the case at Fishlake. Indeed, you will have read on the information board that there are the remains of two crosses in the village, one of which you pass just before the pub.

At the church gate go right, along the signed path, waymarked as the Thorne Round Walk, towards the river. The path leads alongside houses to a stile and then into open fields. Ahead is the big flood bank which obscures all views in that direction. The map shows the path scaling the bank, so you should do likewise. You are now on the highest land for miles. The first of these flood banks were constructed in the 17th century under the direction of the Dutch engineer, Vermuyden. Ostensibly the banks were to improve the drainage and prevent flooding, but in this case something went wrong and whenever the river flooded the water was reluctant to leave. This situation persisted until new flood works were built in the late 1940s.

A glance at the map will show a multitude of single figure spot height figures, for this is fenland, flat as the proverbial pancake, but with a character and beauty all of its own. The map also shows a choice of routes from the top of the flood bank. One descends onto Great Ing and then runs along the other flood bank alongside the Don. In theory this path follows the Don all the way to Hangmans Hill Bridge. You will see from the map that the path makes two crossings of the Don and at neither is there a bridge, though in former times there was a ferry. Thus, in practice, the only choice available is the second path which goes left and follows the main flood bank. When this walk was reconnoitred, Great Ing was full of water in any case and it was frozen. Discretion being the better part of valour, the author kept to the "high" ground where it was relatively dry.

Along the flood bank

The flood bank makes for easy walking and gives good views across the Don towards Thorne. The view is unfortunately marred to some extent by the M18, which is carried over the low lying marshland on an embankment. The noise from the motorway comes as a constant drone, even when you cannot see the road. Surprisingly you cannot see the river at all. It is hidden behind its own flood bank.

[This route appears to be a diversion from the Right of Way; inquiries as to its status should be directed to the Amenity and Recreation Officer, National Rivers Authority, Olympia House, Gelderd Lane, Gelderd Road, Leeds, LS12 6DD]

Ings to the right of them, Ings to the left of them

After about 500 metres on the flood bank, a path falls away to the left to a stile. This is also waymarked as the Thorne Round Walk but your route still lies along the flood bank, though this is not shown on the map as a right of way. To the left is the farmland surrounding Fishlake, not, as you might expect, the prairie style large fields so typical of the Lincolnshire Fens, but small fields, fringed with hedges and mature trees and interlaced with drainage ditches. To the left also lay the Town Ing, whilst to the right is still the Great Ing. Ing is a lovely Norse word meaning an area which regularly floods. As the author walked along the flood bank the were constant creaking, cracking and groaning sounds coming from the ice on the right. An eerie experience. Looking back from this point, there is a very atmospheric view over the village, with the tower of St Cuthbert's sticking up through the trees.

The flood bank begins a long easy bend to the left and the houses of Hangmans Hill come into view on the right. Still the river cannot be seen. Still it is hidden by its own protective bank.

The Don flows home to the sea

At last, as you approach a small brick building on the left, the river finally comes into view. It will come as a surprise to some, though not to anyone who has studied the map, to find that the Don is tidal at this point. Thus you are as likely to be confronted by broad mudbanks as you are by a full river. Nevertheless, you will be

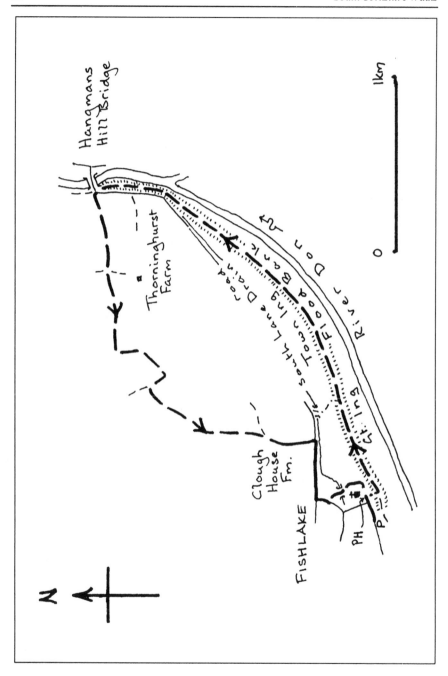

rewarded by the sight of various wildfowl, by gulls wheeling and circling and by a heron or two, patiently waiting for a meal. Adjacent to the brick building, which turns out to be a pumping station, there is a curious stone structure in the field to the right. Closer inspection reveals this to be the remains of a bridge or maybe a sluice, presumably controlling the water levels in the Ing. It is possible to walk alongside the Don at this point, but the flood bank is to be preferred. There are better views and it is drier.

Now the unlovely Hangmans Hill Bridge comes into view and the flood bank path heads towards a stile in the fence at the western end. It is comforting to see that the route you have just trodden merits both a stile and a signpost. Go over the stile and onto the road. Here there is a cross roads. The tarmac route to the left, you should ignore. Likewise the route over the bridge. Instead, go left down the broad green lane, which runs almost due west, away from the river bank. There is a signpost on the telegraph pole to indicate you are going in the right direction.

Ditches and wellies

This section of the walk is totally different from the river bank. There the view was wide. Here the view is very constrained. Trees and hedges border the lane, so that, even in winter you cannot see further than the next field boundary. In summer you won't be able to see through or over the hedges. However, what you lose in views you make up for in the variety of trees, shrubs and wildflowers. The hedges are also home to many species of bird, so there will always be something to see. The lane is broad and as befits a route on this low-lying land, there are ditches at either side. When the author tried out this walk, after the wettest winter for many years, the ditches were full to overflowing and the track was very wet. Indeed, this is one of the few walks where wellies are the recommended footwear. Certainly there were sections where the water would have been well over the top of a pair of walking boots.

Soon you catch a glimpse of Thorninghurst Farm to the left, followed by a new pig unit to the right. A track turns off to the pig unit, but your green lane carries on. It is still muddy and surprisingly for such a seemingly isolated place there are the remains of a wrecked car in the ditch on the left. Soon afterwards, the path turns a sharp left-hand bend by a large willow. Not that there is any chance of you going wrong, as to leave the lane would involve negotiating the ditches, which are quite formidable when full.

THIVES Beware

There is considerable evidence that the track sees use by motor cyclists, but just beyond the right-hand bend there is a series of ruts that no known motor bike could possibly have formed. At the time the walk was surveyed, the ruts were full of water and as the boundary ditches were also brimming over, there was little dry land left. A further right-hand bend means that you have now perambulated three sides of this particular field. Soon you reach a T-junction, complete with yellow waymarker. Go left here, still along a ditch enclosed lane. Beyond the fallen elms, which provide a novel obstacle, or at least a change from puddle hopping, there lie the mortal remains of a bulldozer. The machine is surrounded by a derelict building which sports a notice. This reads as follows, "ARD WILL BE PAID TO ENY WITNES ON CONVICTION OF ENY THIVES ON THIS PROPERTY". Potential THIVES should beware.

Continue along the lane, where the left-hand hedge is now well-trimmed. Soon the church tower of St Cuthbert's can be seen ahead and also a white house. At Clough House Farm there is a junction of tracks and a footpath sign pointing left, across the field. Ignore both the sign and the junction and carry straight on, passing the farm. There is the inevitable collection of farmyard machinery on the right, another target for THIEVES perhaps?

Return to Fishlake

Now the lane becomes tarred and boasts the name of Wood Lane. At the main road, which rejoices in the name of Sour Lane, go right, crossing over to the footway on the south side of the street. Ignore the first turn left, which is a cul de sac, but take the second left, which is Pinfold Lane. After about 100 metres go left along a path across a patch of waste ground. A bridge takes the path over Sour Lane Drain. The path then heads towards the church, with a fence to right and left. At the "crossroads", go straight on, following the path into the churchyard. The vicarage is on the left, a fine rambling building, almost as large as the church itself.

The path skirts round the church to the main gate, where you rejoin your outward route, right outside the Hare and Hounds.

13. Harthill

The Route: Harthill, Thorpe Salvin, Chesterfield Canal, Kiveton Park, Kiveton Colliery(!), Woodall, Harthill.

Distance: 13.5km (8.4 miles)

Start: Centre of Harthill, by the shops GR 494807. Public transport users can either start from Harthill, or from Kiveton Park railway station.

Map(s): OS 1:25000 Pathfinder Series No. 744, Aughton and Carlton in Lindrick.

How to get there:

By public transport: Daily train service to Kiveton Park from Sheffield and Worksop. Daily bus service to Harthill from Sheffield.
By car: Harthill is signed from the B6059 at Wales and from the A618 just north of Clowne and Barlborough. The shops are in the centre of the village.

The Walk

Harthill and the Osbornes

Like so many of our villages, Harthill first appears in print in Domesday Book. The church has the unusual dedication of All Hallows and is worth a visit if you have time. The church contains the tombs of the Osborne family, who were the principal landowners in the area, residing at Kiveton Hall. The Osbornes eventually acquired a dukedom, though they have their fair share of black sheep. The most notorious of these was Sir Thomas Osborne who was involved with various scandals during the reign of Charles II and his successors. Despite his excesses he lived to the ripe old age of 81 and contrived to be buried in Harthill church.

From the bus stop and parking area in front of the Harthill Stores, cross the road and go up Serlby Lane, noting the worn stone walls as you go. The lane bends to the right and then, after about 200 metres, there is a rough track on the left, opposite the garage with the white doors. Go left here to reach a stile and a footpath sign. Cross the stile into open fields and follow the hedge on your left. Where the hedge does a right and left-hand kink, there is another stile, which you negotiate. Carry on, now with the hedge to your right, until the point where the hedge does a left and right kink. Again you will find a stile, again you cross it and still you follow the hedge, though now of course it is again on your left. Note the remains of an old lime kiln to the right, this being confirmation of your suspicions when you spotted the worn walls at the start of the walk. Here you are on limestone. Not the Carboniferous limestone of the Peak District, but the softer, more yellow Magnesian limestone.

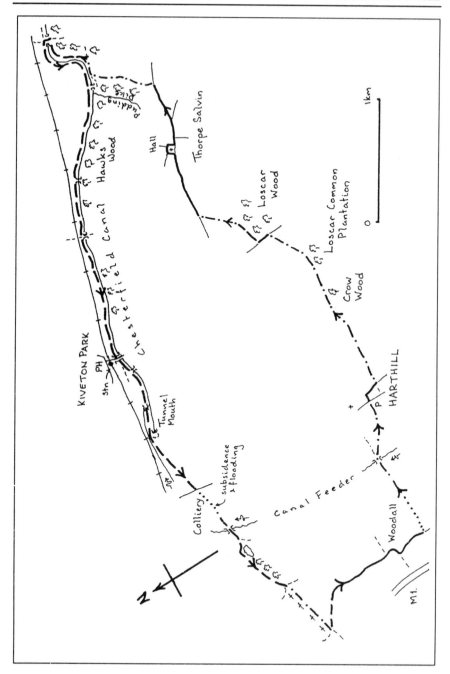

Crow Wood

A stile in the hedge ahead takes you into another field. The path heads across the field towards the left-hand corner of Crow Wood. On reaching the boundary of the wood, the path crosses another stile and runs along the left-hand edge of the trees, before emerging into fields again after about 50 metres. The route now keeps close company with a hedge on your left, heading towards the left-hand edge of Loscar Common Plantation. You have been climbing slightly to this point and looking back there is a good view over to Harthill and Kiveton Park.

When the plantation is reached the path splits. Go straight on, over the stile into the wood, keeping to the left-hand edge of the trees. Unlike many plantations, this one is a fine deciduous woodland. Ignore paths running off to the right, into the wood. Keep to the left-hand edge and soon a stile is reached, which brings you out into open fields again. When this walk was reconnoitred there was a well-hidden electric fence at this point. The path follows the left-hand hedge almost to the end of the field, when it swings slightly right to reach a stile. This deposits you into Packman Lane, opposite Loscar Wood. Older maps indicate a path through the wood at this point, but the newer "Pathfinder" version shows the right of way turning left along Packman Lane. This turns out to be correct. The path is separated from the road by a fence and from Loscar Wood by another fence. The wood is now part of Manor Forest and is private.

Round Loscar Wood

Walk alongside Packman Lane to the end of Loscar Wood and then turn right, through a gateway onto a green lane. This hugs the boundary of the wood as far as another gate. This is the point where the old maps show a path emerging from the wood, but there's no sign of that now. Indeed it does not seem that a path could ever have existed through the trees. At this point there is a signpost, which directs you to the left, across the field. Once in the field, the path heads diagonally to the right, making for the two trees on the skyline. The map shows a number of field names in this area, this one being Loscar Field. These names are obviously survivals of the earlier open field system. The map indicates that Church Field and Lady Field were once much bigger and have been subdivided.

Thorpe Salvin

As you head towards the two trees a footpath sign comes into view ahead, alongside a post which marks the end of the field hedge. This reached, you now turn right along the lane to enter Thorpe Salvin. The village name Thorpe Salvin derives from the common Norse word coupled with a personal name. Notice on the left that the intermediate boundaries shown on the map in Lady Field, have gone, leaving a huge open field in their place. Do not worry about the presence of low flying aircraft, which pass overhead fairly regularly. They are not seeking you out but are taking off or landing at the nearby Netherthorpe airfield.

Take care passing through the village as there are no footways in some parts. Thorpe is a lovely old village. Turn left just before the quaint old church of St Peters, which is worth looking round if you have time. At the next junction turn right and you soon pass the remains of Thorpe Hall on the left, with the new Hall close by. Keep following the lane round to the right to reach the main road again. Here go left, along the road, passing the pump, the Coronation Garden seat and the telephone box. The road rises slightly here and is cut through a band of limestone. At the top of the rise is the village pub, the Parish Oven, on the left. This serves Youngers Beers and food daily. It also boasts a family room.

Beyond the Parish Oven bear left at the Worksop sign, following Back Lane. Go past the playing field on the left and then look out for a footpath sign, which should be alongside the speed limit derestriction sign. Go left here, into fields again, but note the extensive view to the right to Worksop and the Dukeries. Follow the fence on your left until it reaches the corner of Old Meadow Wood. Netherthorpe airfield can now be seen to the right.

Old Meadow Wood and the Pudding Dike

Follow the boundary of Old Meadow Wood. The map indicates a diagonal path going off to the right, cutting off the corner of the field. This path does not exist. Indeed the line of route is well and truly blocked by what seems to be a sewage pumping station. Purists may wish to exercise the rights shown by the map. The author decided to stick to the path by the wood.

The path continues alongside the wood, in which the delightfully named Pudding Dike is visible. At the bottom of the field go right, ignoring the tempting track leading off to the left, down to the canal. This does not seem to be a public right of way, though it obviously sees use. Carry on along the bottom of the field, with a fence and hedge on either side, until you approach Old Spring Wood. The name Spring Wood is very common, but has nothing to do with the watery type of spring. Instead it refers to the type of woodland management. A Spring Wood was one which was coppiced.

Old Spring Wood

Just before the gate into the wood, there is a waymarked stile on the left. This is your route. It cuts through a corner of the wood to emerge, via another stile, onto the track which leads from the gate. The author confesses to missing the first stile, (too much nattering to companions), and using the gate instead. Turn left on reaching the track and follow it as it twists and turns through the wood.

The track is waymarked but not difficult to follow. Any marked deviation to the left would be met by a sudden soaking, for the canal is very close. At one point a path does lead to the canalside, to the top of a lock chamber. The author's long jumping exploits were never much to write about, so a return to the track was advisable. The path continues to twist and turn, following a hawthorn hedge which has gone wild. Where the track forks, by the Old Spring Wood sign, go left to reach the bridge over the canal. Pass over the bridge and go right, descending to the canal towpath. Here turn right again, to pass underneath the bridge, noting the 1835 date-stone in the centre of the arch.

Along the Chesterfield Canal

You are now on the Chesterfield Canal, which despite the date-stone on the bridge is actually one of the first generation of canals, being completed in 1777. It followed the ancient route from Chesterfield to the River Trent, rather than the more obvious course down the Rother valley to the Don Navigation. In part this was to do with antagonism between different waterway companies, in part the influence of land-owners and towns like Worksop, Retford and Bawtry. Either way, the Chesterfield remained isolated from the main canal network, being accessible only via the tidal Trent and having its own peculiar gauge which limited the size of boats which could use it. Despite these handicaps it enjoyed a modest prosperity until the coming of the railways, though its final freight traffic did not cease until the early 1950s. The section east of Worksop remains open for boats, but the great Thorpe flight of locks, the pioneering Norwood tunnel and the Norwood flight are closed and derelict. Happily, restoration is to begin soon.

Walk along the towpath alongside the "staircase" of three locks, which mark the top of the Thorpe flight. From here on, the summit pound of the canal winds its way through beautiful woodland to Kiveton and then to the tunnel. The walk along the towpath really needs no description. However, the phrase "you could do it with your eyes shut", would not be an appropriate instruction. You would end up very wet.

The farm machinery graveyard on the right is soon followed by a bridge over the overflow from the canal. This is followed by a sluice gate, to regulate the water levels in the canal. This canal had the interesting feature of plug holes for drainage purposes. Like your average bath plug, the canal plugs had their attendant bits of chain. Over the years the locations of these plugs had become lost and the tale is told of a gang of British Waterways maintenance men who were dredging the cut. They found a piece of chain and hauled it in, a little surprised to find a piece of rotten wood attached to it. They then adjourned for some lunch and were even more surprised on returning to find the canal empty and their boat high and dry. The sluice is followed by a bridge, which is the one you passed earlier at the bottom of Pudding Dike.

Hawks' Wood and the Devil's Hole

Now the canal runs alongside Hawks Wood on the left whilst to the right the view is more open towards Anston. The remains of old mine and quarry workings can be seen, quite overgrown, but reminders that this canal was built for industrial purposes, to carry coal and stone. Despite appearances now, it was not a rural canal. A number of other bridges are passed, including the ominously named Devil's Hole Bridge and the more mundane Thorpe Bridge. The canal is now closely parallelled by the Sheffield to Retford railway line. It was the promotion of this railway in the 1840s that started the long decline in canal traffic that lead to the demise of the canal. However, the canal company did not give up without a struggle. Instead they turned their company into a railway and canal company and promoted their own line in order to safeguard their traffic. In this they were quite successful, for the combined company ultimately became part of the Great Central Railway, who continued to operate the canal and maintain it until the collapse of the Norwood tunnel in 1908.

On the opposite side of the canal you now pass the remains of a loading dock and a winding hole where the boats were turned round. From this site the Chesterfield Canal Society used to operate a trip boat, but their efforts have since been concentrated on restoration of navigation on the western side of Norwood tunnel, where great strides have been made. For details of the society's activities contact the Secretary at 18 Rosedale Avenue, Chesterfield. S40 2UY.

A visit to The Station

Beyond the winding hole the canal narrows dramatically. Opposite the house there is a stile on the right and a path leading up from the towpath. At the time this walk was being checked, the towpath was inaccessible beyond this point because of rebuilding work to the retaining wall. In any case, you can leave the canal here to visit The Station hotel.

Go through the stile and bear left, climbing away from the canal. The railway is immediately on your right. Where the path levels out you are on top of the retaining wall and the canal is in deep cutting below. Continue along the track until you reach the road. Turn right here, over the level crossing. If you wish ti visit the Station Hotel, you'll find it straight ahead; the station from which it takes its name is on your left. This is Kiveton Park. The *Dictionary of English Place Names* gives Kiveton as deriving from the Old English "cyf tun", which apparently means "a farmstead by a tub-shaped feature"! Quite what the tub-shaped feature is, or was, is not recorded. The addition of the Park is a relatively modern innovation, but Kiveton was recorded in Domesday in 1086 as "Ciuetone".

The Station Hotel

The lure of the "cut"

Retrace your steps over the level crossing. Turn right just before the canal bridge and go along a rough track, with the canal cutting to your left and industrial buildings to your right. Where the track forks, go straight on, by the power line. Soon you cross a bridge which spans a feeder stream to the canal. The way ahead is now no more than a narrow path, with a fence on the left and a hedge on the right. After a little while the tunnel mouth can be discerned below. A path leads off to the left to the tunnel mouth, where there is a plaque giving the dates of opening and closure and the tunnel length. It will be immediately obvious that there was no towpath through this tunnel, all boats having to be legged through. The horses were lead over the top and your route follows the horse path.

Over Norwood Tunnel

Return to the path and go left, noting the numerous water-filled depressions, some of which are on the line of the tunnel. You will also realise that the tunnel is very close to the surface at this point. Modern engineers would have no hesitation in digging a cutting of this depth and it may be that this is the solution to the reopening of the canal, though there are more difficult stretches ahead. Now you can see the cause of the tunnel collapse, for in full view across your line of march is Kiveton colliery. When this walk was being reconnoitred this pit was in full swing and regarded as having a long term future, but by the time the author tapped these words onto the word processor the closure of the mine had been announced, such was the speed on the run down of the coal industry.

The horse route crosses the fields on a path which is paved in some stretches, with the water filled subsidence hollows to the right. These are home to a number of ducks. The path now reaches the road. Here the map begins to look decidedly dubious. There is a stile opposite, leading into a rough area sporting a prominent ditch. The path skirts the edge of the "field" to reach a track, but just beyond that is the toe of the slack heap. This stretches almost to the edge of a pond. Neither appear on the map. A diversion to the left, up the track, turning right just past the sub station, seems to be indicated, but this leads into worse trouble as the path disappears into a very wet field. By wet, the author means water up to the knees, for this field too has been affected by subsidence and a new lake has formed. Again this is not on the map. Therefore, despite the fact that there is a waymarked stile in the far right-hand corner of the field/pond and it is possible to reach it by wading, the author found it easier and drier to squeeze between the foot of the slack tip and the pond. After a somewhat black and muddy passage the path re-emerges as a proper route hedged on either side and well-trodden. At a waymarker post by a footbridge the alternative route joins from the left. Go straight on, over the bridge, which carries the path over the Broad Bridge Dike. This is the main canal feeder stream, running from Harthill Reservoir.

Industrial mess

Follow the path past another pond to emerge into a wholly industrial landscape. The path crosses another stream in which the water is of exceedingly dubious purity, crosses a track which seems to have been used by the entire NATO tank corps and is then faced with a covered conveyor. Thankfully there is a bridge over the conveyor and of course by the time this book is published there may be no conveyor either! You descend from the bridge into another quagmire, but this is of short duration. Follow the good track, which is fenced off from the pond on the left. Ignore the gate on the left, but bear to the right of the grassed and tree-planted mound, which is all that remains of an earlier spoil heap. The next junction of tracks is waymarked and you keep left, with a substantial ditch to the left. The track is rising slightly but nothing to worry intrepid walkers. As you round the end of the tip you can see Wales! I'll leave you to sort that one out.

A three-way split

The track now forks three ways. The broad central way was once the railway branch line that lead from Killamarsh to Kiveton colliery. The path you want keeps to the left of the hedge on the south side of the former railway. This is not quite as shown on the OS map, but it is certainly the walked line. Ahead you can now see the traffic on the M1, whilst to the left is Harthill, your ultimate destination. Continue up alongside the former railway, which soon enters a deep cutting. The line of the path must be almost over the canal tunnel and you are still on the old horse route.

Walseker Lane and Woodall

Shortly you reach a junction of tracks, of which the one you have followed seems the least significant. Go sharp left here, at about a 45 degree angle to your previous route. The track soon develops into a pleasant green lane, tarred beyond the white gates. This is shown on the map as Walseker Lane. It heads direct to Woodall, which was a tiny hamlet, unknown to most people, until the M1 came through and Woodall Services were established. Despite the proximity of the motorway there is surprisingly little interference with the route of the walk, except the constant buzz of traffic.

Ignore the bridleway sign on the left as you approach the metropolis of Woodall and carry on along the lane into the village. At Todds Cottage, which confusingly also has a name-plaque saying Poplar Cottage, there is a footpath signpost on the left and this is your route. The path passes a barn on the right before emerging into a large field. Fix your eyes upon heaven, or at least upon Harthill church tower, for this is the alignment of the path, straight down the middle of the field. Fortunately a kind electricity company has left a couple of pylons in the field with waymarkers on them. Note to the right, Harthill reservoir, which is the supply for the summit pound of the Chesterfield Canal. At the bottom of the field there is a stile in the hedge and a bridge over the canal feeder.

Back to Harthill

On the far side of the stream, bear right, up the field towards the brick house. There is a stile in the top right-hand corner of the field The path then continues diagonally across the next field to a further stile to the right of the fence. Carry straight on here to yet another stile to the right of the fence and above the holly tree. Now bear left, keeping to the right of the brick house to reach a stile in the top right-hand corner of this field. Keep left by the fence to the final stile. This is followed by a quick canter along the lane to emerge by the shops and the bus stop in the centre of Harthill.

14. Laughton en le Morthen

The Route: Laughton, Roche Abbey, Stone, Firbeck, Throapham, Laughton.

Distance: 11.25km (7 miles)

Start: St Leger Arms, Laughton GR. 521881

Map(s): OS 1:25000 Pathfinder Series No. 744 Aughton and Carlton in Lindrick.

How to get there:

By public transport: daily bus services from Rotherham and Sheffield.

By car: from the M1/A57 junction near Aston, follow the A57 to the traffic lights at Todwick and turn left on the B6463. Continue on the B6463 until you reach the B6060. Do a quick right and left at this point, picking up the B6463 again. After about a kilometre take the left turn signed to Laughton. There is plenty of roadside parking before you get to the junction with Eastfield Lane and the St Leger Arms.

The Walk

Laughton village

Despite the picturesque nature of this village and its name, the true meaning is rather less flattering. According to the *Dictionary of English Place Names*, Laughton refers to an enclosure where leeks or garlic was grown. It is from the Old English "leac tun", whilst the rest of the name comes either from the Scandinavian or Old English "mor thing", which means the moorland place of assembly. It is quite amusing to conjure up a picture of an assembly of our ancestors taking place in the middle of an allotment full of leeks! More recent legend has it that there is, or was, a tunnel connecting the church with Roche Abbey. As this would necessitate some three miles of tunnelling, some doubt must be cast on this tale, especially as it was told in the St Leger pub after a jar of Boddies.

At the far side of the pub car park is a signposted gateway into a sloping field. There is a view across the valley of the Hooton Dike to Slade Hooton and the line of the South Yorkshire Joint Railway. As this line was built primarily for colliery traffic, its future must be in jeopardy in the current climate surrounding the coal industry. Follow the hedge on your right until you reach a stile. This takes you into a narrow and muddy field. Go straight across to another stile. Don't use the gateway. You now continue straight on, with the hedge on your right and the Hooton Dike below you on the left. At the end of this field go through a gap on the right and then continue on the same alignment, though now the hedge is on your left. Where the hedge does a crafty right and left stagger, there is a gap through which you pass. The hedge should now be to your right.

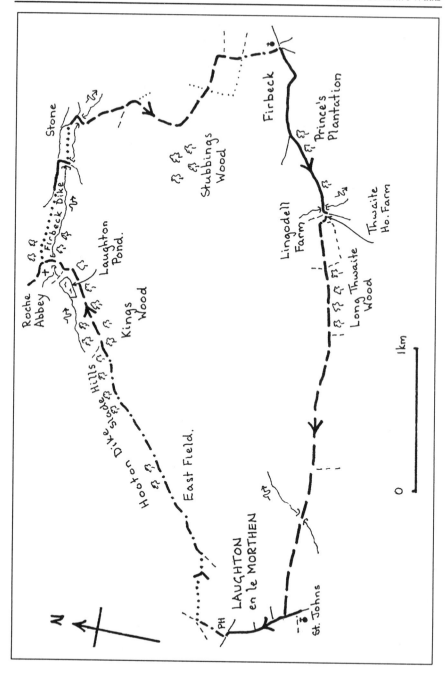

Continue ahead, soon joining a rough lane, where you bear left. There is a signpost for reassurance and a hedge to right and left. On the right is a restored tip, whilst to the left is the steep drop into the Hooton Dike. Where the power lines cross, the lane ceases, but the path continues, now with a hedge to the right only. A path soon bears off to the right, but your route continues on the top of the slope. (The other path isn't shown on the OS map in any case).

Along the edge

A stile is soon reached and then the path continues along the scarp slope, but now with the hedge on the left. From the stile there is a fine view back to Laughton with its magnificent church spire. The OS map shows a series of intermediate field boundaries along the next stretch of this walk, but they have vanished without trace in the race to produce more and more food. A seat has been thoughtfully provided, but intrepid readers of this book shouldn't need a rest just yet, though the view is pleasant.

Continue alongside the hedge on your left. Ignore the track dipping away to the left and continue on top of the scarp. The land falls away quite steeply to the left and is covered with a generous growth of scrub. A real haven for wildlife. Soon the scrub develops into a full blown woodland with holly, ash, elm, oak and beech all intermingled. This is shown on the map as Slade Hills. At a gap in the trees there is another seat and a view across the valley to Colonel's Holt.

Continue to the end of the field, still keeping the hedge and the trees to your left. At the end of the field a stile takes you into Kings Wood. Pheasants seemed to be everywhere when this walk was reconnoitred. A short distance inside the wood you reach a T-junction. Go left here and descend to another T-junction. Here you go right. The path is distinct, but there are various other narrower paths leading off left and right. These should be ignored.

Press before you punch

There are glimpses of a lake to the left, through the branches of the oaks and the dark yews. The path follows the remains of a wall on the left. Look out for one of those curious trees with the very soft bark that you can pummel with your fists. Make sure you get the correct tree before you try. The author will not be held responsible for any fractured wrists or fingers!

Roche Abbey

The path now drops to the left, to a set of stepping stones over the weir from Laughton Pond. Just before the weir there is a signpost and a path to the right. This is your route. Now you get your first sight of the ruins of Roche Abbey, and very impressive they are too. The name "Roche" comes from the Norman French and means "rocks". As you near the abbey the reason for the name becomes obvious, because the ruins nestle against an outcrop of limestone. Continue along the path, now with a fence to the left. Cross the bridge and stile, from which there is a good view of the abbey. Continue alongside the fence, passing to the east of the ruins. As you near the crags, there is a signpost. Those visiting the abbey should go left here. Those whose

Roche Abbey

thoughts are on more earthly things, like getting back to the St Leger before closing time, should go right.

The OS map shows the footpath running along the base of the crags and the bank, but there is little evidence of use. A broad cart track slants up the bank to reach the wall by the road. When this walk was reconnoitred, there were some very frisky horses in this field and the author decided that the track was better, as it gave the opportunity to escape over the wall onto the road. Both track and path converge near Abbey Mill Farm, where there is a stile by a gate. This takes you out onto the A634 Maltby to Blyth road, close to the bus stop.

Go right at the road, and in less than 100 metres, you go right again, leaving the main road and descending quite sharply along a little lane. Just by the farm and before the bridge, there is a footpath sign on the left and thus you reach green fields again. The path now runs alongside the Firbeck Dike, with incipient limestone crags on the left and woodland on the right. Near the end of the field, the path is forced upwards to the left, to reach a kissing gate in the top corner by the crags. The gate lets you out into a narrow lane and here you go right.

Stone Green and the devious route to Firbeck

The narrow lane descends to Stone Green where the garage has the original version of a natural stone roof. At Stone Mill, turn right and cross the bridge over the Firbeck Dike. Go past the mill and bear left up the track. This climbs steadily away from the stream, past a fine beech tree. The track soon bears away to the right, but go straight on here, through a signposted gateway, into fields. Follow the way marker, which takes you to the right of the hedge, then head diagonally across the field towards the signpost on the far side. Here you pick up a good track again and bear left. The track follows the field boundary on the right, but it is soon obvious that this route is not as shown on the OS map. The map shows a bridleway heading straight across the fields towards Firbeck church, which can be seen ahead, but the track bears right alongside the hedge and there is no sign of the direct route. Fields boundaries have been grubbed out here with gay abandon and there is little choice but to follow the good track as it makes for Stubbings Wood.

About 200 metres short of the wood, the track forks and the main route goes left, down the hill, heading towards Firbeck church. Part way down the hill, the track does a slight left-hand kink. This marks the spot where the direct route shown on the map should cross. There is no evidence of it on the ground, so carry on along the track, which soon bends round to the right and reaches a junction in the middle of the field. Go straight on here, still making for the church along a good track. The track soon finishes, but an obvious path continues, making for the right-hand end of the church. As the outskirts of the village are reached the path is walled and fenced on either side, running past the church yard on the left before dropping down a flight of steps onto the village street.

A saintly author?

As you look at the church you will realise that the author is in exalted company, for the dedication is to St Martin.

Turn right at the foot of the steps and make your way through Firbeck along New Road. The road soon describes a tight right-hand bend, followed by an equally tight left hander. Be careful as there's no footway at this point. Note the attractive house, dated 1876. The windows are particularly fine.

Thwaite House and Wood

Once past the bends, there is a ditch on the left-hand side, which is lined with a wall. Soon the lane forks and your route lies straight on, alongside the tree belt of Prince's Plantation. The spire of Laughton church soon comes into view on the right as the lane begins to descend to Thwaite House bridge. Once over the bridge, at Thwaite House Farm, there is a minor cross roads, more of a cross tracks really. The lane you have been following goes sharp left, but you go straight ahead, following the footpath sign. The track soon swings to the left and there is a gap in the boundary ahead. Despite there being no signpost, your route lies through this gap, then to the right along the bottom of the field, behind the house. In a very short distance, less than 100 metres, you reach a hedge, which hides a lovely little green lane. Here go left and follow the green lane up between the hedges until you reach a "cross roads" at the corner of Long Thwaite Wood. Carry straight on, with the wood on your left and open fields to your right. At the top corner of the wood, a track goes off left, but your route lies straight on, heading for the bush on the brow of the hill. Laughton spire soon comes into view again and forms a marker from now on.

Aspire to St Johns

Beyond the brow of the hill there is a signpost and the path soon assumes the proportions of a rough lane again. It soon becomes obvious that the path is tending away from the seductive spire of Laughton church and is heading instead for the squat tower of St Johns. Ignoring all tracks and paths leading off right or left, the track pursues an unerring course for almost a kilometre, to a bridge over a small stream. Beyond the bridge the track resumes its course, now upwards, by a ditch and hedge, to a short length of green lane, which emerges on the main road close to St Johns church. The church is now abandoned and in a sorry state, despite being in the "care" of the Redundant Churches Commission. It must have been an attractive building at one time, but the church yard was unkempt and rubbish strewn when the author visited. The position of the church is curious as there are very few houses anywhere near. A glance at the OS map will show that the parish of Dinnington is no more than one field wide at this point and just takes in the church yard. All around is Laughton parish, but Dinnington's official parish name is Dinnington St John.

From the sorry remains of St Johns, make your way up the road, back to your car, the bus stop, or the St Leger.

15. Lodge Moor (Sheffield)

The Route: Lodge Moor Bus Terminus, The Sportsman, Redmires Conduit, Redmires Plantation, Redmires Conduit (north), Headstone, Reddicar Clough, Wyming Brook Drive, Fox Holes Lodge, Three Merry Lads, The Sportsman, Lodge Moor Bus Terminus.

Distance: 9km (5.6 miles)

Start: Public transport to Lodge Moor is so good that it seems almost criminal to give directions by car. As a compromise the walk starts from the bus terminus rather than the car park.

Map(s): OS 1:25000 Pathfinder Series No. 743 Sheffield.

How to get there:

By public transport: Frequent daily services to Lodge Moor from Sheffield City Centre.

By car: There are innumerable ways to Lodge Moor from the various parts of Sheffield, but the most obvious is via the A57 to Crosspool church, then turn left, (signed to Lodge Moor). Follow this road for a little over 3 km until you pass Lodge Moor Hospital on the left. Continue on past The Sportsman and the Three Merry Lads for about a kilometre to the car parking area at Wyming Brook GR 269858.

The Walk

The leaving of Sheffield

From the bus terminus, walk up the road, away from the city, towards the Sportsman. Even for a public transport user, 400 metres must be considered poor justification for stopping for a pint, so at the pub, turn left along the signed footpath. This takes you along the side of the pub and past the outbuildings to reach the playing field. There is a view across the Rivelin valley from this point to the distant Hoober Stand and Keppel's Column.

Make your way across the playing field, between the pitches. At the far side of the field the cared for turf of the playing area deteriorates into rough grass. The path winds through this, with the wall on the left. A T-junction is reached and here you should turn right. This is the eastern arm of the lengthy Redmires Conduit. The water channel itself is to the left, though it isn't up to much. There is a seat on the right, which would be ideal for those who have ignored the author's advice and stopped already for a pint or two of Directors. For stronger minded souls, carry on along the conduit path, passing the wood on the right. At the end of the wood, the view northwards opens out, but on the left is an enormously high wall. Why anyone should

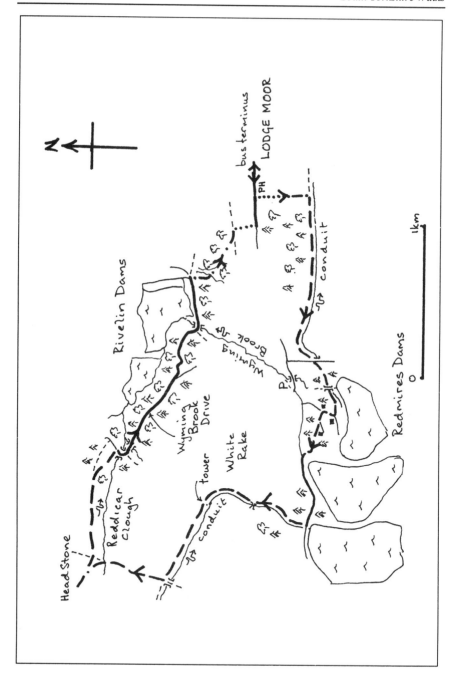

wish to build a wall of such a height is a mystery. The path passes through the wall at a convenient gap.

A grand waymark

To the north you can make out that grandest of all Yorkshire waymarks, Emley Moor television mast. There is another seat thoughtfully provided, but for some inexplicable reason, it doesn't face the view. A stile takes the path out onto Soughley Lane. (Car users should turn right here and go down the lane to the T-junction and there turn left to reach the car park). Cross the lane and go over another stile almost opposite. This takes you into what appears to be a walled green lane, but it isn't. The walls mark the boundary of the waterworks land and in between the conduit is covered. After about 100 metres of green lane, you reach a gate. Here the conduit construction is obvious, for the arching can be seen where this small occupation bridge spans the watercourse. Another gate takes you back onto the green lane and this is followed to the wood.

Go through the stile into the wood where the conduit runs as an open ditch to the left of the path. The waterworks buildings can be seen to the right, through the trees. A further stile leads onto a rough and muddy path, which descends steeply, below the wall of the lowest of the Redmires Dams. At the bottom the path joins the reservoir road where you turn right, through the gateway. The signs advise you to "Follow the waymarks". Follow the road, between the buildings and then turn left at the T-junction. This is marked by a blue signpost. Carry on up this road until you come to a gate. Another blue sign indicates that the route is to the right, not through the gate. The path follows the boundary of the waterworks buildings, hemmed in on both sides by fences. On the right, notice what seem to be an odd series of brick built boxes. What purpose did they serve? The path soon reaches the trees and winds through them, with glimpses to the second dam, to the left. A footbridge over a stream leads to a stile and thus onto the road. Here you go left. (Car users will join at this point, having simply strolled up the road from Wyming Brook).

Redmires Conduit and the Headstone

Walk up the road for about 400 metres, until you are level with the top dam. Here a path goes off to the right alongside the conduit. The path is signposted and there is an information board describing the area. This conduit is radically different from that you saw previously. This one is almost wide enough to be a canal and it carries a considerable volume of water. Its length is five km, but only two km. can be officially walked, which is a great pity as it offers an opportunity to reach the northern end of Stanage Edge, without road walking. Walk along the well-graded path which soon emerges from the trees to give a grand view back towards Lodge Moor and down the Rivelin valley. The path runs slightly east of north, contouring round the hillside. The construction of the path, the walls and the bridges is substantial. Good honest gritstone that looks totally at home here on the moors. Continue through a series of gates, never leaving the side of the conduit. The path now swings to the northwest, passing a squat, stone built tower. This was used for surveying the conduit. From the top, both ends of the watercourse can be seen and the requisite fall calculated. As the path heads for the north west, the various rock formations on Derwent Edge can be seen on the skyline. Nearer, just to the right, and only just visible, is the rock tower known as The Headstone or Stump John.

At the next bridge a path comes across from the Redmires Road and bears away northwards towards the Headstone. There is a gate across the conduit at this point, for this marks the limit of public access. Turn right and, leaving the conduit descend across New Hagg Moor, with the wall to the left. The frequently muddy path descends through the heather, keeping close company with the wall. Where the wall swings away to the left, the main path continues straight ahead, but a narrow track bears away left, still quite close to the wall. Follow this track and the Headstone soon comes strikingly into view. The view up the Rivelin valley from the Headstone is quite striking. Even more striking is the contrast when you turn towards the city, for then you can see just how close this area of near wilderness is to Sheffield.

Leave the Headstone and follow another narrow path towards the tower at Lodge Moor hospital. The path is often obscured by heather and after heavy rain you can expect to get wet legs here. Soon the path reaches a cross "roads", where you rejoin your original route from the conduit. The crossing is signposted and you should go straight on, along the ridge known as Headstone Bank. Rivelin Reservoirs are now in view ahead and the path descends gently towards them. To the right is Reddicar Clough, an area of scrubby trees and bracken. Shortly the path forks. The right of way descends to the right, into the clough. The other fork, which is not shown on the map and is not a right of way, continues along the ridge top before descending steeply through the trees to reach the reservoir road. Of the two, the ridge top route seems more regularly used, but the right of way is the correct path, and it avoids the scramble down to the road.

Reddicar Brook

At the road, turn right and cross Reddicar Brook on a substantial bridge. Follow the reservoir road round the bend until you reach a junction. (If you have come by car and have had enough of this walking lark, you can reach the car park very easily from here, by bearing right and walking up Wyming Brook Road). There is an ancient signpost at the junction directing you to the Manchester Road and Moscar. Your route lies along the left-hand fork. The road now begins to descend towards the lake, which can be glimpsed through the trees on the left. At the point where the road levels out, there is a cluster of stone buildings on the left. These mark the exit from the Rivelin Tunnel, which brings water from the Derwent Dams, under Stanage Edge. The outfall lies to the left, a little further on, another grand piece of Edwardian civil engineering by a progressive group of local authorities. The outfall reaches the lower lake at the same point as the Wyming Brook and this is crossed by a stone bridge. The road now runs alongside the lake and is a popular stroll for the residents of Sheffield.

Danger! Sewage?

At the reservoir house, known as Fox Holes Lodge, the road passes through a gate and swings left to cross the dam wall. Just before the road goes left, there is a footpath sign on the right accompanied by a stile. Go over the stile and then head up the right-hand path, with the lodge just to your right. The other path is the more obvious, so be careful. The path you want is graced by a sign proclaiming, "Danger Sewage, keep to path". The reconnaissance party decided that this was a much more effective method of preventing trespass than the usual "Private Keep Out" notice. Certainly we stuck rigidly to the path as it twisted and turned its way up through the trees. Keep the stream to your left, until the waymark indicates the crossing point. Another stream is soon reached and crossed and the path continues upwards at an easy gradient, through the trees, but there was no sign or smell of sewage. All too soon the path steepens and takes off to the right, up a stony slope, aided in parts by steps. There is an indistinct crossing of paths, where the path you want is fortunately the most obvious. It continues upwards. A final pull lands you on top of the ridge, with a fine view back to the reservoirs and eastwards, down the valley.

Go left at the main path and then, almost at once, bear off to the right, climbing a narrow path for a short way until the playground of the Three Merry Lads comes into view. The path passes through the grounds of the pub to reach Redmires Road, where you turn left. The Sportsman pub is about 250 metres further on the opposite side of the road, whilst the bus terminus is about 400 metres beyond that.

16. Longshaw

The Route: Longshaw, Fox House, Houndkirk Moor, Blacka Plantation, Wimble Holme Hill, Totley Moss, Longshaw.

Distance: 8.5km (5.3 miles)

Start: Longshaw Car Park GR266800 (for car drivers) or the Fox House Inn, for public transport users.

Map(s): OS 1:25000 Pathfinder Series No. 743 Sheffield, Outdoor Leisure Series No. 2 The White Peak.

How to get there:

By public transport: daily services from Sheffield, Bakewell, Buxton and Castleton. Seasonal services from Chesterfield and Dronfield.

By car: Follow the A625 from Sheffield, signed to Castleton. Just past the Fox House turn left onto the B6055, following the signs to Longshaw Country Park. The car park is just on the right. It is manned and currently costs £1 for all day, supervised parking.

The Walk

Farewell Derbyshire

From the car park in Longshaw Country Park, which is in Derbyshire, make your way towards the visitor centre. At the first junction, take the path to the right, which emerges just opposite the Fox House inn, at the road junction. Continue along the A625 in the direction of Sheffield. Ignore the footpath signs and at the chevron bend marker, bear left along Houndkirk Road, which is a rough track, signposted as a bridleway. There is now a good view back, over the Fox House, into the heart of the National Park.

At the cross roads go straight on, through the gate, which is signposted as a by-way. This serves to remind you that Houndkirk Road is open to vehicular traffic, not just walkers and horse riders. You are quite likely to encounter motor cycles and maybe even an intrepid four wheel drive exponent, but they are unlikely to cause any trouble. Houndkirk Road was originally a turnpike route out of Sheffield until the present A625 was built. As such it retains its vehicular use rights and the usual turnpike width between boundary walls. Continue upwards, ignoring the sign on the left tempting you to Open Country and the footpath sign to the right which doesn't feature on the OS map at all. Notice that the fields to either side are reverting to heather.

A tremendous view

Just past the small standing stone on the left there is a tremendous view back over the Peak District and to the right over the Rother valley to Chesterfield and beyond. Now the track begins to level out and where it does, the view ahead and to the right expands tremendously, reaching to the Trent valley. Test your knowledge of the Trent power stations. How many can you see? The author reckons six, but how many can you name? To the left you can see Burbage and Stanage Edges, with Derwent Edge beyond.

Now the track dips and runs over a small embankment, held in place by a dry stone retaining wall. Ignore tracks to the left and right and continue along Houndkirk Road until you reach a crossing of tracks, marked by a signpost. Here a narrow path leads off to the right, waymarked by a yellow arrow on an upright stone. Follow this path, which is distinct enough at first, but which rapidly deteriorates as it finds its way across damp, boggy ground. Head just to the right of Houndkirk Hill and you will not go far wrong. The path skirts to the right of the main wet patch, eventually reaching a solitary post at the foot of Houndkirk Hill. From the post a distinct path materialises again, descending to reach the head of a small valley. The A625 road and its by-passed predecessor can be seen below, but the path does not take the obvious course of descending the valley to reach the road. Instead it keeps high up and contours away to the left, before descending quite sharply to reach the main road close to its junction with Whitelow Lane.

Devil's Elbow Gate

Go through the kissing gate, choosing your companion with care, descend the steps and then cross the road to reach the footway. Now go right for about 250 metres, passing the Peak National Park boundary sign. The remains of the old road can be seen to the right, making a tight bend round the head of a small valley. The later A625 strides confidently across this minor obstacle on an embankment. On the left-hand side of the road you now reach a wood and shortly afterwards there is a gate on the left, with a signpost saying "Bridleway to Shorts Lane". This is the Devil's Elbow Gate, the devil's elbow in question being the by-passed piece of old road you saw earlier.

The path descends through the lovely mixed woodland of Blacka Plantation, soon reaching a junction of tracks within the wood. These boast an array of signs that would do credit to the M1 and which are quite out of place in this setting. Continue downhill, through the wood, noting with concern that the walk started at a relatively high point and has been descending for some considerable time. A long climb is therefore in prospect. The deciduous woodland turns to pine and larch as the track comes alongside a small stream. This is one of those cases where the stream seems to favour the path rather than using its own bed, so in normal English summers, this could be quite a damp stretch. A very wet patch heralds the approach to the Blacka Dike. Another track joins from the right and again there are copious signposts. Go left here, crossing the side stream on a bridge. At the next T-junction, go right and descend to the Blacka Dike, crossing it on stepping stones. The path climbs steeply away from the stream, up a flight of steps.

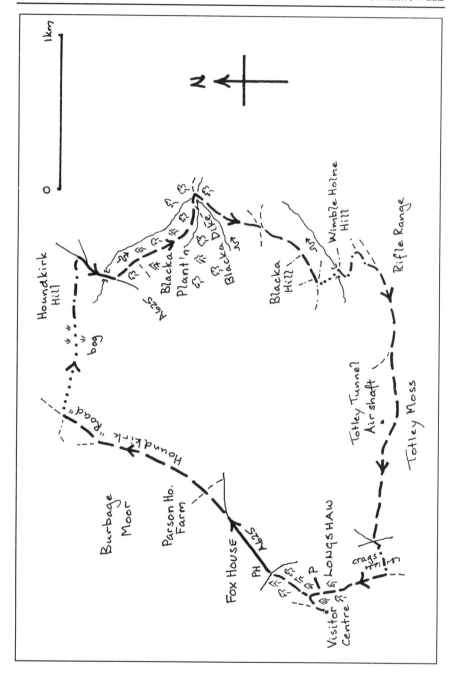

Onwards and upwards

Still climbing sharply through a delightful woodland, the path crosses a bridge over a tributary stream. Beyond this point the wood begins to thin and eventually opens out completely. Ignore the path going off to the left and carry on upwards, on an easier gradient. Soon you reach a major junction of tracks. Go straight on here, past two posts. There is an unexpected view to the left over to Norton. You had no doubt forgotten how close you were to Sheffield. Here is a reminder. Pass the seat on the right, or use it if you feel the need, then carry on up the well-defined track. Ignore the decrepit sign on the right and the more readable signpost. These only lead back to the main road.

To your left the clough deepens and falls away steeply from the track. Carry on up the path ignoring further tempting paths on the right, until you reach a gate by a clump of trees. You are now on the Outdoor Leisure Map. The map indicates that the path carries on across the field to a junction at the far side. By turning left at the junction you would then follow another path back across the same field but diagonally this time, thereby completing two sides of a triangle. Not surprisingly, there is evidence on the ground that walkers reaching the gate by the trees, turn left by the fence and wall and simply go down the short side of the triangle to a railway sleeper bridge at the bottom.

Beyond the bridge, a gate leads onto the moor. You are already in the Peak National Park, but here you enter the Park's Eastern Moors Estate, whilst the bridge marked the boundary between Sheffield and Derbyshire. The path forks just inside the gate and you go right, following the fence cum wall. The path then turns sharp left up the hillside and you have to scramble up the steep flank of Wimble Holme Hill. The good view down the valley is a perfect excuse to stop for a breather, but in truth the climb is not long and you soon reach the top. Here the path levels out and soon dips to join another, larger track. This is one of the many variants of the Totley Moss Road, an ancient right of way from Sheffield over to the Hope and Derwent valleys. Go right here, passing the warning notice which reminds you of the potential dangers of tangling with gun toting men. Soon an even wider, more well-used track is joined and here you bear right, following the road up onto the moor top.

Over Totley Moss

The tall post on the left displays a red flag when there is shooting at the nearby range, but the right of way is supposedly sacrosanct. Soon you see ample evidence of the use of this "road" by 4 wheel drive vehicles. There are some massive ruts, which could easily drown an unwary walker who fell into them in wet weather. The use of this route by vehicles has become something of a "cause celebre" recently, with the Derbyshire County Council having to undertake considerable maintenance works to make the road passable. Unfortunately it was found that the used line did not coincide with the definitive map line (What a surprise!), so there were quite complicated legal manoueverings to regularise the position.

Continue across the moor, noting the air vent for Totley Tunnel on the right. When the railway was being built in the 1880s and 1890s the Duke of Rutland, who owned the land forbade the construction of the usual number of air-shafts for fear they would ruin the grouse moors. This vent is one of the very few on this tunnel. Ahead you will see the mast crowned summit of Sir William Hill just overtopping the moor.

The track now forks and here you keep left along a freshly stoned section of path. This is one of the sections rebuilt by Derbyshire after the ruts had become too deep even for 4 wheel drive comfort. Imperceptibly you have now come over the high point of the moor and an increasingly extensive view opens up ahead. Far to the south you can make out the tuft of trees on the top of Minninglow. Also in view is a wide sweep of the Derwent valley, swinging round into the Hope Valley and the Vale of Edale. The curious wooden pole away to the left is a guide post marking the course of an old pack horse route.

Longshaw Estate and tea

Continue ahead along the track. The rocky tors beyond Fox House now come into view to the right, Higger Tor and Carl Wark. Your route now reaches a gate just at the junction of the two main roads. Cross the road to reach another, smaller gate, which lets you into the National Trust's Longshaw Estate. Note the curious crater like depressions on the left, probably the remnants of old quarry working. Owler Tor and the Hope Valley are clearly in view from this point, but the path soon reaches the edge of a line of low crags. A stone staircase, part natural, part man made, descends through the crags to reach a broad track. Here you go right, and carry on along the track until it forks. Go left here, though the gate into the wood, heading towards the visitor centre. The path joins the main route from the car park at a big stone guide post. The car, bus and pub are to the right. However, the visitor centre is worth a visit before you leave, so now would be a good time. They also do an excellent cup of tea in the cafe. What greater temptation could there be?

17. Low Bradfield

The Route: Low Bradfield, Blindside Lane, Andrew Wood, Dale Dike, Strines Reservoir, Foulstone Delf, White Tor, Cartledge Stones Ridge, Abbey Brook Head, Dukes Road, Hurkling Edge, Agden, Rocher Head, Agden Reservoir, Kirk Bridge, Low Bradfield.

Distance: 19km (11.8 miles)

Start: Low Bradfield Car Park. GR 362920

Map(s): OS 1:25000 Pathfinder Series No. 726, Sheffield (North) and Stocksbridge, plus Outdoor Leisure No 1 The Dark Peak.

How to get there:

By public transport: Low Bradfield boasts a daily service from Sheffield, and not just one bus a day either.

By car: The only route worth trying to describe is that from Malin Bridge. Follow the B6077 from its junction with the A6105, all the way to Low Bradfield. Turn right at The Plough, then over the bridge, straight on at the next junction and finally, right along an unsigned lane which leads to the car park. There are at least half a dozen other ways to reach Bradfield but these are best left to the locals.

The Walk

The Bradfields

Bradfield is a huge parish and contains a number of settlements of which the central ones are High and Low Bradfield. The usual derivation of this place name is from the Old English "brad feld" which means a broad stretch of open land. The South Yorkshire version of this common name is no exception. The Bradfields, Low and High, were first recorded in 1188 as "Bradesfeld".

The Bradfields are set in the Peak National Park, in that part known as Sheffield's Lake District. Until a few years ago the local bus company ran tours to "The Lake District", for the princely sum of 50p. Pity any ignorant soul who expected a visit to Windermere!

Leave the car park by the access road and at the junction turn left to go down to the bridge which leads into the village centre. Carry straight on at this point, with the picnic site to the left and cross the other bridge, over the Dale Dike. The road now begins to climb towards the Plough Inn. Just beyond this, go right, along a signposted track beside the water treatment works. This works deals with water from the three reservoirs upstream of this point, Agden, Dale Dike and Strines. The tarred lane turns to a rough track after the cottages and narrows still further after a gate and stile. Ignoring the gate to the left, carry straight on along an obvious path. A stile by

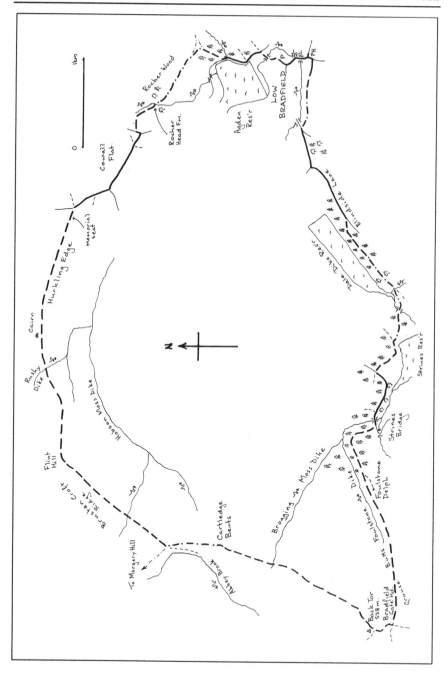

an oak tree leads almost at once to a bridge over a small stream. The path continues under trees before emerging into open fields. A view opens up the valley to Thornseat Lodge, high above. Your route takes you even higher!

The path now bears right to reach a stile by the gate and thus you regain the road.

Alas poor haychatter

Go left along the road, but not up the lane to Doe House. The lane now begins to climb steadily, with views to the left over to the Haychatter Inn. The lane is fringed by larches and hazels. When we investigated this walk there were hazel nuts scattered alongside the road. One of our party pronounced that the nuts had been nibbled by dormice, but not surprisingly we never saw any.

Safe haven by Dale Dike

The road swings sharply to the left at a junction. Still rising, the road now bends to the right and soon reaches Brooms Cottage. To the left the land rises sharply and breaks away into crags. To the right the road is lined by trees, but do not go into the wood at the first access. Carry on instead to the footpath sign which leads into the wood. Inside the wood there was evidence of nefarious activities. Two safes lay in the undergrowth with their doors blown off. If you are walking through these woods and hear loud explosions, you now know what to expect. The trees mask the reservoir below except at a few places where you catch a glimpse of the water. This is the infamous Dale Dike Reservoir. Its infamy stems from a fateful night of 11th/12th March 1864, when the dam burst sending a flood of death and destruction down the valley into Sheffield. 240 people were killed. There is an information board telling you about the reservoir and its wildlife just inside the wood.

Continue on the good path through the wood. Soon you will catch a glimpse of the curious tower on Ughill moors. The path emerges from the wood at a gate and stile. Here there are waymarks to the left and right but your route lies straight ahead across the field on a pronounced terrace. About half way across the field, the path bears away to the right to a gateway. Pass through this and carry straight on, with a wall to your left, until you reach a stream. Cross the brook and at the next gateway bear right before carrying straight on across the next couple of fields until you reach another stream. This you cross by a plank bridge.

Strines Reservoir

The map shows the path forking at this point, but this doesn't happen in practice. Instead an obvious path leads up, from the stream, bearing right, to come alongside a wall. Follow the wall until you reach a stile on the right. Negotiate the stile and you come into water company property. The path drops to river level through a riot of bracken and soon a bridge is reached. Beware rotten planks! Having safely crossed the bridge, continue up the obvious path through the pines. The dam of Strines Reservoir can be seen to the left, along with the Ughill tower. A stile takes you out of the trees and into the open again. You should see Brogging House ahead and the path makes for this. Climb the brief steep slope up to the stile near the house and then skirt round to the right of the buildings to reach a track. Go left here. Brogging is a reservoir keeper's house, but he also seems to keep a variety of livestock as well. Follow the track past the house, through a belt of trees, beyond which you get a vista of the Derwent Moors and the various rock outcrops crowning the tops. When the walk was reconnoitred the heather was in full bloom and the moors were a glorious sight. Strines Reservoir lies to your left. It was almost totally dry when the author made his visit.

Follow the track up to the road and here go left. Ignore the tempting stile opposite, leading into the wood. This is a permissive path designated by the Fitzwilliam estate but although it starts off in the right direction, it doesn't end up where you want to go. You must use the road instead, so be very careful, especially at the right-hand bend. In contradiction to the usual dictum that you should walk on the right of the road, you are probably safer in this case to walk on the left. At least there is a verge here on which to leap in emergency!

Strines Bridge?

Continue down the road and across Strines Bridge. Interestingly, although the OS map describes this bridge as Strines Bridge, the stream it crosses is not the Strines Dike. The stream of this name is crossed about 150 metres further on. Strines Bridge would appear to cross Holling Dale Brook, or it might be Foulstone Dike, or even Brogging Moss Dike, or maybe again Rushy Flat Dike. None too clear on the 1:25000 map! Still arguing this technical point with your companions, don't miss the track going off to the right, about 100 metres beyond the bridge. This is Foulstone Road and it is the route you want.

Foulstone Road, so called, is a rough track that is passable for four wheel drive vehicles and is used by such for access to the shooting butts higher up. It is one of the few public routes onto the moors from this eastern side, but it runs through a jealously guarded grouse moor, so no deviation from the path. The climb is quite steep initially, passing through the conifer plantations. After about 7 or 800 metres you reach a gate, which sports a notice telling you in no uncertain terms who owns this land and that you must stick to the path. Beyond the gate lies open moorland and the gradient eases.

Foulstone Delf

To the left, a track leads away to the shooting lodge of Foulstone Delf, but the main track and the public path parallel the steam, though well above it. Soon a line of grouse butts comes into view on the right. The path continues to rise and the grouse butts seem to converge towards it. Your suspicions are soon realised, for the line of butts is seen to come right across the path and continue on the southern side. Where they cross, there is a good view back over Bradfield and also the beginnings of a view to the south towards Stanage Edge. A colleague of the author's has experienced difficulties on this path in the shooting season, receiving polite but firm requests to turn back or wait until shooting has finished. For the record, the landowner is not allowed to stop you from using this route so that shooting can take place. Indeed he is under an obligation to ensure that shooting does not interfere with the public right of way and certainly under a duty to ensure that members of the public using the right of way are in no danger from the guns.

Bradfield Gate Head

Carry on up the path which gradually levels out as the crest of the ridge is approached. The various outcrops of rocks on Derwent Edge come steadily closer and look more and more exciting as they are approached. Suddenly, at a crossing of paths the view widens to encompass the whole of the high moors of the Peak. A vast expanse, taking in Kinder Scout, Bleaklow, the Axe Edge Moors beyond Buxton, south to Sir William Hill and even tree crowned Minninglow. A great swathe of the Derwent valley is visible to the south, guarded on the left by the gritstone edges. You have reached Bradfield Gate Head. The gate element of this place name has nothing to do with your average garden gate. It is another word for a road. The Bradfield Gate was thus the route leading to Bradfield.

Turn right here and make your way up the path to the trig point on Back Tor. The edge path roughly marks the boundary between Fitzwilliam land, to the right and National Trust land, to the left. You can wander at will on the Trust's land, but not on Fitzwilliam's. At the trig point you are on one of the highest points on the Derwent Edge and the view demonstrates this graphically. The author was blessed with a superb day when reconnoitering this walk. From Back Tor you could see Lincoln Cathedral with binoculars, and Emley Moor and Holme Moss television masts without. It says a lot for the decline of South Yorkshire's heavy industry though.

From Back Tor follow the path in a north easterly direction, first descending from the summit rocks and then across the broad and boggy expanse of Cartledge Stones Ridge. There is no doubting where the path runs, for it shows as a broad quagmire across the moor. Marker posts are not there to guide your feet to drier parts, but to delineate the boundary between the Trust and Fitzwilliam lands. Needless to say, the path treats this boundary with contempt, being more concerned with dry feet. There is one particularly delightful spot, where an enticing green sward turns out to be a quaking bog. Unless you want the ground to move for you, pass this by to the right. After about one and a half damp kilometres of this, during which time you concentrate far more on the ground, or lack of it, under your feet, than on the view, a little knoll is reached. This is Cartledge Bents. It is dry enough and pleasant enough to sit down and contemplate the folly of ever buying this book. It would also seem from the map that it is in Fitzwilliam territory, despite the obvious path.

Abbey Brook and the Dukes Road

Cartledge Bents overlooks the deep valley of the Abbey Brook. Beyond the valley and to the left lies Howden Edge and Margery Hill. Coming up the valley and crossing the moor just below where you sit, runs the Dukes Road, another ancient trackway from the Derwent valley over to the Don. Leave Cartledge Bents, heading towards Emley Moor Mast. The narrow path soon disperses in the mire as the bog is reached again. There are wooden posts along this stretch but they are of no help in route finding, though they might help you float in extreme cases. Having crossed

Carledge Bents, Derwent Moors

this moor on many occasions, the author can vouch for the fact that nothing short of a six month drought, or a three week cold spell at -20C makes any difference to the quagmire. Soon the head of Abbey Clough is reached and here there is not bog but a stony waste. The path from Cartledge Bents meets the Dukes Road at a big cairn.

(A narrow path continues ahead and can be followed up the Cartledge Brook, right onto Howden Edge and Margery Hill. Unless you have plenty of time and stamina, this is not recommended, though the views from Margery Hill can be excellent, (we could see York Minster and the Wolds on our visit). It is necessary to retrace your steps to the head of Abbey Clough in any case).

Assuming you're not going to Margery Hill, turn right at the cairn and the RRW boundary stone and proceed along the Dukes Road. This well-defined path rises gently across the heather moor, before levelling out on the flanks of Bruston Croft Ridge. The way is cairned or marked with stakes and boulders. The higher land to the left masks the view in that direction, but to the right there is a fine vista. See how many power stations you can count.

At Flint Hill, the path, which has been running in a north easterly direction, turns almost due east and begins to descend quite sharply. This change in direction is marked by a cairn, though it is scarcely necessary. Now the path is almost on the ridge top, so there is a view both sides. There is the inevitable Emley Moor mast, but on a good day the Yorkshire Wolds can be discerned far away to the north east. The vegetation on the moor gradually changes as you descend. Here and there are odd thorn bushes, wind battered and sheep bitten, but still clinging tenaciously to life. The track dips to cross the bridge over the Rushy Dike stream. Shortly after the bridge there is a large cairn on the left, just off the track. This has no apparent significance, though there is a good view from this point, including the new windmills near Penistone. Now the right-hand side of the track is marked by a dry stone wall, but there is still a view down the valley to Damflask and Agden Reservoirs. A further steady descent on a good path along Hurkling Edge soon leads to a cluster of rocks. From here there is an excellent view down the valley. There is also a seat from which to enjoy it. The plaque on the seat is in memory of Helen Dunn, who, it says, "loved the wild high places". She chose well. Beyond the Dunn memorial seat the path passes through a kissing gate to reach a track down to the road.

The Rocher

At the road go right, ignoring the track which leads off to the left. Go down the hill, passing Mortimer House on the right. This shooting lodge gives its name to the road as well. At the first road junction go left along the nearly level lane. The tower near Ughill, which you saw earlier in the day is clearly visible on the opposite side of the valley, whilst ahead is a prominent rock outcrop known as The Rocher. This is a place name you have met before. It derives from the Norman French and simply means "rocks". It is fairly common in South Yorkshire, but its most impressive manifestation is The Roaches, in Staffordshire. As you approach the end of this lane, the road begins to rise and there are footpath signs to the right and left. Neither are on the 1:25000 map. Carry on to the T-junction and there go left. There may be dissension in the ranks at this point, for the road signs at the junction clearly indicate that Bradfield lies to the right. Fear not, but believe in the author.

After less than 100 metres on this road, go right, passing through a gate into a narrow walled lane. There is a footpath sign marking the route. The lane, which is no more than a rough stony track, descends to Rocher Head Farm. The route through the farm buildings is waymarked. Beyond the farm the track becomes merely a little used path as it enters open fields. There are the remains of a hedge on the right and the path runs along a well-defined terrace, with view down to Agden Reservoir. Close scrutiny of the OS map implies that the path should be on the other side of the hedge, but this is clearly not the case in practice. To the left can be seen the tumbled boulders and crags that gave The Rocher its name. The way ahead lies over a ladder stile in the fence on the right by the holly bush. (Ignore the more obvious stile and path going off towards the rocks). Beyond this, all semblance of a path vanishes, but you should bear left to locate a stile that is cunningly disguised in a bit of wall. This proves to be an awkward beast to negotiate, just when you thought you were on the home stretch.

Bootless and blinded we hopped back to Bradfield!

In the next field the path bears right, across a steep slope. On of the reconnaissance party lost a boot at this point and finished the walk with one stockinged foot! We ended up at the hospital that night with the same person. However, the cause was not bad feet but grit in the eye. A dangerous place is Bradfield. The path splits in this field, but both routes lead to a gate. Beyond the gate the path turns sharp right and descends the slope, by the wall to a waymarked gate and stile in the bottom corner. Again, this is not quite as shown on the map. Pass through the gate or over the stile, depending on the amount of energy you still have left, and enter the wood. A rough track descends, damply, through the wood to emerge on the road at a gate and stile. Agden Reservoir lies just over the wall at the opposite side of the road. Turn left here and follow the road for about 500 metres, past the dam and past the house with a blue gate, alongside which there is a footpath sign on the right. Go right here and descend the narrow walled and fenced path. The path is steep enough to warrant steps in places. It crosses another track and continues down more steps to a bridge over the Agden Dike. Cross the bridge and go left, alongside the stream on a paved path. This is perched somewhat precariously above the river in places, but there are no problems. Ignore the next bridge on your left, instead bear right to reach a stile into the car park.

18. Micklebring

The Route: Micklebring (Well Fm), M18 Bridge, Micklebring Gorse, Firsby Hall Farm, Conisbrough Parks, Park Lane, Conisbrough Lodge, Micklebring Gorse, M18 Bridge, Micklebring.

Distance: 8.5km (5.3 miles)

Start: Layby opposite Well Farm GR 514948

Map(s): OS 1:25000 Pathfinder Series No. 727 Rotherham

How to get there:

By public transport: Bus services from Rotherham find their way into Micklebring, with a stop near the Plough.

By car: Anyone passing along the M18 will know Micklebring and the Plough Inn. It is prominently in view on the left as you descend from the limestone cutting in a south bound direction. It is equally prominent on the right as you ascend from Junction number 1. It is less easy to find than to see. You should leave the M18 at junction number 1 (the A631 turn) and take the A631 eastbound for a short distance, before turning left into what seems to be an industrial estate. Micklebring is not signed at this point. The road winds through the estate, eventually joining Old Hellaby Lane. This soon runs close to the M18 before reaching a junction with Moor Lane at GR 507941. A quick right and left here – the visibility is not of the best, takes you into Greaves Sike Lane. This is signed to Micklebring. About a kilometre along this lane look out for a large layby on the left, opposite Well Farm. If you pass the Plough you've gone too far.

The Walk

Micklebring

The name Micklebring has an obscure derivation. The first part is either Old English or Old Norse and usually means "large". The remainder of the name would appear to include the common "ing" element which usually implies a place "belonging to", except that in this instance there is no obvious personal name included in place name. It may on the other hand, be a corruption of "spring", in which case the name simply means, the large spring. If this is true, then never was a place more aptly named, for this was a decidedly wet and muddy walk.

After admiring the extensive view from the layby, walk up the lane towards the Plough Inn. There is no footway so take great care, though the road is fortunately lightly trafficked. Pass the pub and continue up the lane until the Manor House is reached on the left. A footpath sign points left, apparently over a wall. There may have been a stile here at one time, but not now. Use the adjacent driveway instead and then pass to the left of the bungalow to reach a flight of steps. Go down the steps to a stile. This should drop you neatly into open fields, but it doesn't. Instead the path has been fenced off from the field and you are hemmed in between a wall on the left and the fence on the right. Another stile and then a fine collection of ex railway fruit vans. Beyond these there is a fence to left and right and no escape until another stile is reached by a sleeper bridge. Once over this you are at last into open fields. The path continues unfettered, bearing right, by the hedge to reach a stile in the bottom corner. The M18 is now looming ahead and has to be crossed. No difficulty here, for there is a bridge under the motorway.

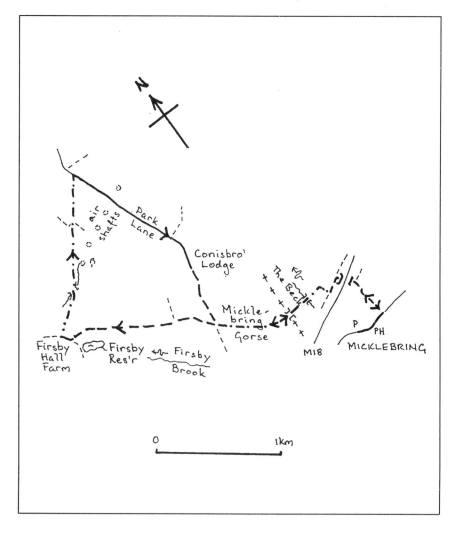

Under the M18

Beyond the bridge go left along a track, ignoring the footpath sign on the right. There is a wide view to the right, including Hoober Stand. It is quite remarkable how often this crops up in views from all angles. Whilst you are looking at the view, don't forget to keep your eyes peeled for a stile in the fence on the right, about 150 metres from the bridge. The stile is way marked but unsigned. Go over the stile and into the field. Bear left here along a sketchy path, heading towards a gate in the left-hand boundary about 100 metres along. Take care not to end up in the ditch! There is another way mark at the gate and the path goes left, into another field.

Unusual fence posts

Once in this field, go straight ahead to a waymarked post and there bear right, around a patch of scrub. The path is now distinct again, heading straight across the field towards the obvious brick walls. These turn out to be the parapets of a bridge carrying a farm track over a now abandoned railway line. Go over the bridge. The cutting is quite deep, but heavily overgrown. Go through the gate at the far end of the bridge and come into fields again. This is Micklebring Gorse, except that there is no gorse to be seen. Indeed, it looks as if the whole area has been scoured clean of all natural vegetation and then replanted with one type of grass. Hedges have been replaced by new barbed wire fences, but these are not without interest. The uprights are former telephone and electricity posts, some still with their insulators and pole numbers still attached. Conisbrough Castle can be seen to the right and inevitably Hoober Stand gets into the vista.

The path descends by the fence before rising again to reach a more prominent hedged track at a crossing of paths. Follow the route straight ahead, marked by the footpath sign. This passes through a gap in the hedge into open fields again. Bear right in the field, heading towards the slight dip in the horizon. An electricity pole soon comes into view and is a useful marker, a fact confirmed by the presence of a proper way mark just to the left of the pole. The path now runs alongside a hedge on the right, with Firsby Hall Farm in view ahead and Firsby Reservoir on the left. Further to the left is the tower of Ravenfield church, with its little spire.

The weight of the world on his boots

The next section proved to be one of the muddiest walks the author has undertaken for some considerable time. After five minutes it felt as if the entire weight of the world was fastened to his boots. Certainly most of the contents of the field seemed to be clinging tenaciously, unwilling to be torn free from the ground and equally unwilling to be shaken free from the boots.

At the gateway follow the track straight on, with the hedge now on the left. Another gateway takes the muddy track out onto the farm road by Firsby Hall. Right here, noting the farm gateway left with its carved faces. Where the farm road goes left, rounding the end of the buildings, there is a stile on the right and a footpath sign. This field also proved a trifle damp. The path bears right, alongside the hedge to reach a waymarked stile. Once through this stile, bear left, following the hedge and stream. The view to the right includes the television mast on Beacon Hill, just north of the M18.

Abandoned mine shafts

Continue alongside the stream to an old sluice gate. The map shows a field boundary here, but it doesn't exist. Follow the stream to the left and then to the right, along the edge of the field, noting the curious clump of trees in mid field and the grass grown hummocks that march in a line up the hill. The map gives the clue, for these are old mine shafts, from former colliery workings, now long abandoned.

Pass over the culvert on the left and then go right, to reach the waymarked post to the right of a waymarked tree. A plank bridge spans a hidden ditch and in the next field the path bears left to clip the corner. The old shafts are now clearly visible to the right as is the Plough, standing proudly on its hilltop. At the far end of this field there is a hiatus. You join a track which quite is clearly signed as Private, no public footpath. Equally clearly, the map shows a public right of way. The clue is to follow the track ahead, not left. Where the track swings to the right, there is a footpath to the left, over a culvert. The path then strikes diagonally right across the field, heading for an orange waymark on a post. The path is well-defined in any case. At the waymarker, the path squeezes through a gap in the thorn hedge onto Park Lane, where you turn right.

The status of "white" roads

The original intention of this walk had been to proceed via Park Farm Cottages and Conisbrough Parks Farm, but this route, which appears on the map as a white road, is clearly signed as private. It is high time the OS indicated the status of these white roads, because some are private and others not. The relevant information is usually held by the local highway authority, so there's no real excuse.

Mud and peacocks

Park Lane is no more than a track. Bowl steadily along towards Conisbrough Lodge, admiring the extensive views. Clifton village can be seen to the left and the Plough is also in sight. Looking back you can see Conisbrough Castle and there is an unusual view along the Don valley towards Doncaster. The line of old shafts is crossed and soon the low drone of traffic on the M18 can be discerned. Ignore the footpath sign on the left and continue ahead, through a gateway onto a proper lane and Conisbrough Lodge Farm. The author's notes for this farm state "mud and peacocks", which constitute a pretty memorable combination. You'll have difficulty in avoiding the mud, but the peacocks make up for it.

Pass through the farm and out onto a lane again. The lane is hedged on both sides as it climbs away from the farm. At the fork in the lane go left and continue ahead, over the brow of the hill until you reach a footpath sign on the left. Go left here a rejoin your outward route. You shouldn't need any further description to complete the walk, unless you are suffering from very rapid memory loss, but for completeness here goes.

Speed the (muddy) plough

Descend across Micklebring Gorse before rising to the gateway and bridge over the railway. On the far side of the railway, bear left towards the post by the clump of hawthorn. The path is obvious anyhow at this point. Bear left at the post to reach a gate and culvert over a stream. Then bear right, heading towards the waymarked stile and a good track. Left now, to reach the bridge under the M18. The author's notes just say "dry", which is probably the highest accolade anyone has ever paid to this bridge. Just beyond the bridge go left at the stile and then immediately right, alongside the hedge, not straight on over the more obvious stile. Follow the hedge up to reach another stile on the left, taking care at this point not to end up in the ditch. The path then leads up through the fields, past the railway vans to the bungalow and the main road. Go right to reach the Plough and the layby.

19. Norton (near Askern)

The Route: Norton, Norton Priory, Norton Mill Lane, Willow Bridge, Little Smeaton, Womersley Park, Womersley, Womersley Beck, Birdspring Wood, Walden Stubbs, Tanpit Bridge, Norton.

Distance: 12.75km (7.9 miles)

Start: Norton Priory GR 544158 for car users, Public transport users alight at the School Boy pub.

Map(s): OS 1:25000 Pathfinder Series No. 704 Hemsworth and Askern

How to get there:

By public transport: there is a daily service form Doncaster and Pontefract.
By car: The easiest way to find Norton is from the A19. It is signed from the junction about 1.5km north of Askern. If you arrive by this route, drive past the School Boy Inn and then go right at the cross roads, by the Royal Hotel. After 0.5km, there is a triangle of land at a T-junction. Cars can be parked here. It is possible to reach Norton from the A1 at Barnsdale Bar by following the signs to Askern. Once off, and over, the A1, look out for signs on the left for Norton. In Norton, go left at the Royal Hotel.

The Walk

Norton and its Priory

Norton was, of course, mentioned in Domesday Book, but there is evidence of much earlier occupation. The church is dedicated to St Mary Magdalene and boasts some very fine medieval stonework, including the magnificent tower. Almost certainly this is simply a rebuild of a much earlier church, maybe even a Saxon foundation. Assuming you have arrived by bus and have got off at the School Boy, walk along the main street until you reach the cross roads by the Royal Hotel. Go right here, up the narrow lane, which is Priory Road. Although at first the lane is hemmed in by buildings it soon opens out once Back Lane is passed. Continue straight on for about another 300 metres until the T-junction is reached at Norton Priory. Car users will start from here.

Go left at the triangle, with Norton Priory on your right, behind the wall. This was one of the victims of Henry VIII's activities and very little now remains of the priory, except the mill and farm buildings. The narrow lane bends first to the right, then to the left before reaching the mill buildings. A footpath sign indicates a route to the left, but this is no use unless you have a burning desire to return rapidly to Norton. Instead, carry on along what now becomes a track and soon enter open fields. The track is Norton Mill Lane. After a couple of hundred metres along the lane there is a signpost on the left. This you ignore. A short distance further on is a footpath sign on the right and this is your route. The map indicates that the footpath crosses a strip of water, presumably the old mill pond. This does not exist. Instead the path crosses a flat field to a bridge over the River Went. Again, this is at variance with the map. The map shows stepping stones at this point, but thankfully these have gone. Accessing them down the steep bank would have been at best difficult and at worst very wet!

A devious departure from the Great Republic

Cross the bridge and enter North Yorkshire, leaving the Great Republic behind. Turn left and follow the path along the river bank. About 150 metres along the bank you reach a stone gatepost. The path clearly continues along the riverside, but the map indicates that the right of way bears off to the right, diagonally across the field. There is no evidence that this route is ever used though North Yorkshire county council confirm that it is still the right of way. Indeed, on the hillside, where the path should be, there is a new(ish) structure, well-fenced. The author followed the beaten path by the river.

The odd gateposts are almost the only remains of removed field boundaries. The map still shows the old fields and is quite confusing. The walked path follows the river as it bends to the right. A line of scrub and trees mask the river as the path nears the corner of the field. At the end of the field, by the large willow, the path becomes indistinct and crosses over a shallow ditch. Thereafter it bears left and heads diagonally across the next field to a waymarked stile in the far hedge. This field was very wet when the reconnoitre took place, but it had been the wettest winter for some time. At least the path wasn't completely flooded.

Willow Bridge and the Hull and Barnsley

Once through the stile, bear left towards a blue gate in the bottom corner of the field. The tree covered embankment which forms the boundary of the field is the course of the old Hull and Barnsley Railway. This line opened in the 1880s as an attempt to break the North Eastern Railway's monopoly in Hull, but closed in the late '50s. At the gate, which was well-guarded by geese when we passed by, there is also a stile. This gives out onto a track and thereby onto the road at Willow Bridge. The railway must have crossed the road and the river on a very skewed bridge, of which only the bases of the piers remain. The drive on the right leads up to the old station, now a private residence. Go right at the road and then left at the junction, following the signs to Kirk Smeaton and Wentbridge.

Follow the hedge lined lane which climbs steadily upwards. There is a pleasant view along the valley to the tower of Kirk Smeaton church. At the scissors cross roads in Little Smeaton you go first left and then right, just missing the Fox Inn. This tempting-looking Bass house has a lovely view across the river.

No Hoober Stand!

Leave the Fox with regret and continue the climb out of Little Smeaton. As the brow of the hill is reached, Eggbro' and Drax power stations come into view on the right. The extent of the view is quite surprising, but we looked in vain for Hoober Stand,

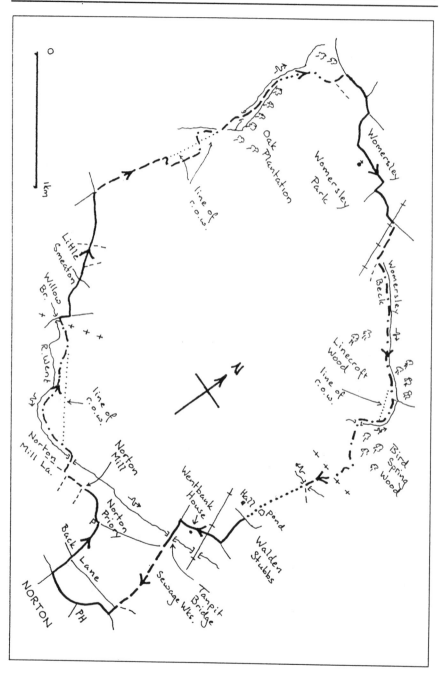

which seemed to crop up in every view elsewhere in the book. Ignore the waymarked gate on the right and the stile on the left. Instead, continue along the lane until you pass the houses on the right and reach a cross roads. The right-hand arm of the cross is a mere track and this is your route. The track rises away from the cross roads and soon Ferrybridge power station comes into view. As the track tops the rise and begins to descend there is a view ahead to Womersley church spire. Indeed this is about the best view you get of the church, because it is screened by high walls once you are in the village.

Another deviant path

The track dips quite steeply, running down between hedges and heading towards Oak Plantation. The map indicates a line of trees stretching out to the right of the wood, but these have all gone. The track stops abruptly at a field boundary bank. The map, true to form, indicates that the right of way carries straight on and the county council confirm this is the case. Indeed one of their own walks leaflets gives directions along this path. No one seems to have heeded this, for there is no evidence that the direct route has been tackled. Instead there is a beaten path going right, following the bank and hedge. The boundary soon swings left and continues the course towards Oak Plantation. Follow the patchy hedge for about 300 metres and then stick alongside the bank as it swings left. Roughly 100 metres along this bank there is a large thorn bush. This seems to mark the point where the right of way should emerge according to the map. There is no evidence to suggest that it has ever been tried. Again, theoretically, you should turn right at this point and go diagonally across the field, heading towards the gap in the far hedge, about 100 metres up from the wood. The walked route seems to follow the boundary, turning right at the field corner and the following the hedge down to the gap. The gap turns out to be a snare and a delusion, for it is protected by a deep ditch. A little further on there is a single plank bridge spanning the ditch, and a waymark to prove you are on the right track. Care on the bridge, which is slippery when wet!

In the next field, bear right to clip the corner and reach the tip of the wood. Here a two plank bridge, also waymarked, spans an even deeper ditch and takes the path over into the wood. At first the path follows the stream on the left-hand edge of the wood, but soon the waymarks direct you to the right. The path twists through the trees, some of which have waymarks on them, until you emerge on the far side. Here the path goes left to follow the edge of the wood, cutting through a tongue of scrub which isn't shown on the map. At the end of the field there is a waymarked stile and plank bridge. Beyond this obstacle the path is virtually none existent. Bear right towards the hedge and continue alongside it where it swings to the right. The map now shows the path sticking close to the hedge, but on the ground at this point a track materialises, running slightly to the left of the hedge. Whether you choose to follow the hedge or the track, either way you will end up in a quagmire at the far end of the field. The stream which has run to your left from the point where the track was joined, now seems to have deposited its entire contents over the path. Negotiate this as best you can – it's marginally drier nearest to the hedge and fence. Ignore the track going straight ahead through the gate into Icehouse Park. Instead, bear left over the culvert to pick up a decent track, which runs between walls, up to a gate and stile.

Womersley

Once over the stile, turn right and go along the road to enter Womersley village. Womersley is a delightful little village with some charming buildings. Like its near neighbour, Norton, Womersley is a much more ancient place than it seems at first, probably predating Domesday by many centuries. The road skirts the boundary walls of Womersley Park on the right, On the left is the village school. Cow Lane and Park Lane lead off on the left, but ignore these, following the main road through the village. Just near Park Lane, note the new development with the roofing mimicking the local speciality of mixed stone slates and pantiles. To the right now you should see the church, but you can't because of the high walls of the Park. To the left there is a craft and herb centre and then the road swings sharp right to a T-junction. Go left here, following the signpost to Whitley. Soon you pass the Manor House on the left, a fine looking building and then suddenly you leave the estate village behind as you reach the level crossing. The old station, closed now of course, lay to the left. The station house is still there and a fine spot it is too. Very grand. Go over the level crossing and then at once turn right, along a track beside the railway. The track is signed as a footpath.

More deviations

After about 300 metres, the track crosses a culvert over the Wolmersley Beck. An indistinct track carries on beside the railway, but the footpath turns left to follow the beck. The stream had been well and truly dredged out when we passed that way, so there was little sign of any wildlife. Hopefully it will recover. Beckclose and Limecroft woods can be seen to the right, whilst ahead is Brown Ings Wood. As Brown Ings is approached, the path crosses a brick culvert over a subsidiary stream and then continues alongside the beck until the tip of the wood is reached. The map would now have you believe that you bear right at this point, making a bee-line for a point about 100 metres to the right of the edge of Birdspring Wood. This does not happen in practice. Users of this path follow the stream edge, beside Brown Ings Wood until the plank bridge is reached. Do not cross the bridge, but continue alongside the stream until you reach Birdsprings Wood. Still following the stream, the banks of which show every sign of being about to collapse, so steeply have they been cut, you soon reach a single plank bridge. This is waymarked! Go across the bridge taking care not to fall into the ditch, and follow the edge of the wood for about 400 metres. At this point you reach a field boundary. There is little or no evidence of a path, but the route lies to the right, away from the wood, but alongside the hedge.

After a short distance there is a gap in the hedge and a well-defined track leads past a tip on the left. A surprise at this point is a well-built bridge, which used to carry the Hull and Barnsley Railway over the track, but now carries nothing over anything. The track rises to cross the old railway embankment and then descends to field level again. The map shows an ancient moated structure in the field on the left of the track, but you'll need the trained eye of an archeologist to discern it. Follow the track across the field to a bridge over a stream. Across the bridge the track carries on, but your route lies to the right, through a gap into another field. Follow the left-hand hedge, with some trepidation, for there is no evidence that anyone has passed this way before. However, at the end of the field there is a single plank bridge over a shallow ditch and a gap in the hedge beyond, which gives you some confidence. Carry on with a hedge and ditch to your left. Stubbs Hall can now be seen ahead. Confidence rises still further when at the next fence there is a stile. Keep on alongside the hedge on the left until you reach the wall which surrounds Stubbs Hall.

A damp approach to Walden Stubbs

Pass through a gap in the wall on the right, leaving the ruined building to your left and skirting to the right of the pond. Once through the wall keep left and head for the stile which will let you out into the road. You will almost certainly find your way barred by a stream, which is not shown on the map and which is not bridged. It can be crossed be deviating to the left and by some agile tussock hopping. The path is not at all clear at this point, and the description of the route through this last section doesn't really accord with the dotted green line shown on the map. However, it does seem to be the only way through and until someone waymarks an alternative it is offered to those intrepid walkers who venture into this border country. In this manner you reach the hamlet of Walden Stubbs.

From the stile go across the road and straight on down the lane opposite. In about 400 metres this turns sharp right and so reaches a level crossing. Go over with care and continue along the lane until you reach a T-junction, just past Wentbank House. The map shows a footpath continuing straight on at this point, but those of you who are looking for a short cut back to Norton Priory and your car will be sadly disappointed. There is no indication of a path or even a sign. Instead, go left at the junction, noting the base of the old wayside cross in the triangle of grass. The lane now descends a little to Tanpit Bridge, which spans the River Went and takes you back into South Yorkshire. Border formalities were minimal and we returned to the Socialist Republic without difficulty.

Back to School

About 150 metres from the bridge the lane swings to the right. If you are set on returning direct to your car, simply follow the lane for a further half kilometre back to Norton Priory. Those whose thoughts are more on School Boys and drink should carry straight on along the rough track. The charms of the local sewage works are revealed on the left, but these are soon passed and you proceed along Stubbs Lane, through the fields until Back Lane is reached. Here you are on the outskirts of Norton and the track becomes a tarred road leading down to the main street. Turn right at the main road and in about 300 metres you reach the School Boy. Cross the road with care and sample the brew.

20. Penistone

The Route: Denby Dale station, Hagg Wood, Upper Denby, Clough Dike, Tanyard Brook, Ingbirchworth, High Lane, Royd Moor Reservoir, Bell Royd, Top o' th' Town, Thurlstone, Bridge End, Penistone station.

Distance: 9km (5.6 miles)

Start: Denby Dale station GR. 274084

Map(s): OS 1:25000 Pathfinder Series No. 715 Barnsley and Penistone

How to get there:

By public transport: Both Denby Dale and Penistone have a daily train service from Sheffield, Barnsley and Huddersfield, plus daily bus services from the same places and Holmfirth.

By car: Although the walk starts at Denby Dale you need to park in Penistone and catch the train. The A628 road runs through Penistone. The B6462 crosses the A628 at Bridge End. If you are coming from the west you should turn right at the B6462. If you are coming from the east you should ignore the first junction with the B road and continue over the bridge to the second junction where you turn left. The station is signed from the B6462.

The Walk

Not a meat pie in sight

After a very pleasant ride on the train, alight at Denby Dale station. The station exit dives down under the line in a subway, then goes left, alongside the viaduct. When the road is reached, go left, passing underneath the viaduct. The viaduct is a curious structure. There is the usual series of arches to take a double track railway, but on the west side there is an additional section, which stops abruptly. The explanation for this curious feature is that the original viaduct was a timber trestle structure, approached by two stone arches. The trestle was demolished in 1884 when the present stone viaduct was built, but the two original arches remain to this day.

Oh, for a path across the viaduct

Once through the viaduct, cross the main road and almost at once turn right, down a lane, which looks as if it is a private access. It isn't. This lane takes you almost back to the viaduct again, but then, on the left, is a bridge over the River Dearne. Over the bridge, turn left along a track by the stream to reach the cottages. The track continues as a surfaced lane, up to Back Lane where you turn right and begin to ascend quite steeply. It is at times like this that you wish that the local authority had prevailed upon British Rail to allow a path alongside the railway, over the viaduct. Continue upwards until you reach the main A635 road. Here turn right and once again pass underneath the railway. Immediately on the far side of the viaduct, there is a track on the left, signed as a bridleway. Go left here and leave the road behind.

Into Upper Denby

The bridleway ascends steadily, with Hagg Wood on the right. For quite some way the route is stone paved, a sure sign of heavy historic use. It is also a wet and muddy climb after, or during, heavy rain, as we found to our cost. At the top of the hill there is an excellent view to the north east, over Denby Dale. The track continues to a cross "roads", where you go straight on, still following the bridleway. This soon swings left and becomes a tarred road as it enters Upper Denby. Keep straight ahead, ignoring any junctions, until you emerge on the B6115, just opposite Peter Holmes' stores. Here turn right, and walk along the main road for a short distance, passing the telephone box. At the school sign, cross the road and go left, along the driveway, which is signed to Ingbirchworth. A gate at the end of the driveway leads into fields and there is a view across to Ingbirchworth and the 13 windmills. Continue along the path with a wall on the left and fence to the right. The path descends now, with new planting on your left. This section was extremely wet and muddy when checked, a situation not helped by construction works which were obviously going on in the adjacent field. The track drops down alongside a stream on the left until a waymarked gate is reached. Just beyond the gate, the stream dives under the track, or at least it is supposed to. Anyone who feels in urgent need of a bath at this point need look no further, for there is a large enamelled example alongside the track on the right, fed by a stream.

Goodbye West Yorkshire

The path, now of cart width, drops steeply down into Swift Wood where it bears left, following the line of the stream. A culvert takes the track over the Clough Dike to another waymarked gate and thus into open fields again. The track is fenced on both sides as it rises across the fields. Soon, almost in mid field, you reach two gates, both of which were closed across the track when we were there, rather like a level crossing gate being closed across the railway. The explanation is that cattle graze the fields on either side and are allowed free access between fields, but not along the bridleway. The railway line to Penistone is visible to the left. The track again dips towards a stream, fringed with trees. A bridle gate launches you out onto a slippery clapper bridge, spanning Tanyard Brook. It also spans the county boundary, for this is the point where you leave West Yorkshire and enter South Yorkshire.

A misleading "waymark"

Up you go, along a pleasant hollow way. At the top the hollow way clearly carried straight on, but the present right of way goes through a waymarked gate on the right, then turns left alongside a wall. The windmills are much more obvious now, to the right. Continue along the track, through two waymarked gates. Do not go through the third gate, despite the waymark, but turn right instead, still on an obvious track. In less than 100 metres there is a stile and a footpath sign on the left. Leave the track at this point and go into the field. There seems to be a large yellow waymarker on

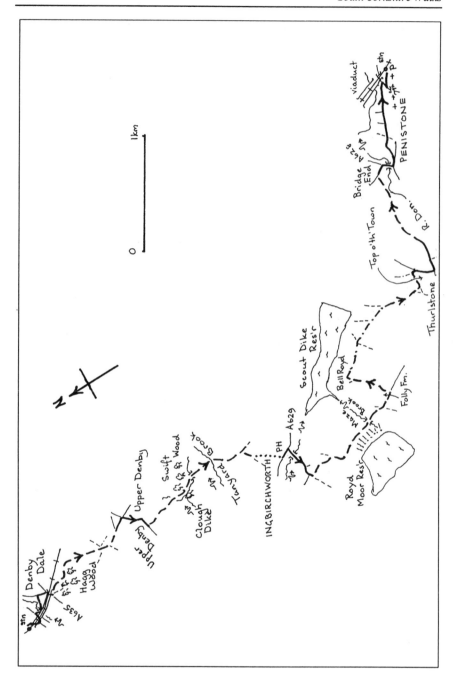

an electricity pole in mid field. Closer inspection shows this to be nothing of the sort. Instead you should head for the red brick bungalow and thus you will find a stile by a gate. Cross the next, very narrow, field to another stile in the far wall. Over this, and follow the wall on the right to a further stile which seems to land you in someone's back garden. The path does a dog leg through the garden to reach a stile onto the main road. The Rose and Crown is just to the left.

Ingbirchworth

Ingbirchworth enjoys what might best be described as a bracing climate. Certainly on our reconnoitre the wind speed can only be guessed at. For all that it is an attractive little spot, though the main road spoils it somewhat. The records suggest that had you done this walk half a century ago, you'd have had three pubs to choose from, but no matter, the Rose and Crown is good enough for anyone and you may wish to stop off here.

On leaving the pub, cross the road and go right, down New Row Lane. This dips sharply to cross the stream, before rising again towards Broadfield Farm. Note the sign with the name, Ing Field. There is nothing missing from the name. An "ing" is an area of land that frequently floods. Carry on up the lane to the point where High Lane bears away to the right. Go straight on here, following the Camping Club sign. At the footpath sign go left, but not through the gate. The path is narrowly contained between stone walls. The windmills come into view again on the right, whilst to the left is the usual farm machinery graveyard. The path is paved and this is a sure sign of antiquity and previous heavy use. Soon the view to the left opens out to include Scout Dike Reservoir and further away the welcome tower of Penistone church.

Royd Moor Reservoir

The path edges its way along the foot of Royd Moor Reservoir dam. You never see the reservoir itself, but it lies to your right. Try not to think of what would happen if the dam gave way!. The path descends steeply to cross the outfall from the reservoir. This section and the next portion, are contained in classic hollow ways. As you top the rise, there is a view to that grandest of guide stones, Emley Moor mast. A track joins from the house on the left and an enticing footpath sign indicates a route to the right. Ignore these blandishments and carry straight on along the rough lane until you reach Folly Farm on the left. (If time presses, you can continue ahead here, along the lane, which leads directly to Thurlstone). Go left here, down the rough track to Bell Royd Farm. The view ahead is extensive, and as ever there is the game of "name the power station" to be played. Bell Royd Farm has a date plaque of 1776 in the wall. The path does not go into the farmyard, but passes to the right of the garage to reach a ladder stile. Continue ahead until you reach another ladder stile and here you go right, into open fields. One of the author's companions was trying out the new fangled "ski" poles, which are supposed to ease the strain on your knees. After attempting these two ladder stiles the conclusion was that the poles were a xxxx nuisance!

Of bulls and mud

Continue ahead, alongside the wall. There is no obvious path, but the route is not much in doubt. A stile takes you through to the next field and the path still follows the wall. Another ladder stile follows. More cursing from the pole bearer. The path now briefly joins a track, which bears left into a veritable quagmire of a field. Follow the wall on the right as best you can. The farmer has dumped lorry loads of rubble in what looks like a vain attempt to raise the ground above water level. Unfortunately, no-one has seen fit to spread the lorry loads so they remain in piles. This made for an interesting passage, especially as there was a bull in the field at the time of our visit. A combination of driving rain and a field full of cows meant that the bull was not interested, which was fortunate, as the combination of mud and roughness meant that any attempt to run would have been difficult in the extreme.

At the far end of the morass, there is a stile in the wall. A more obvious track goes through a gate but this should be ignored. Go through the stile and continue ahead with the wall on your left. Ignore the stile in the wall on your left, by the large gatepost. Instead, bear right here, go across the field and you will then spot another stile in the far right-hand corner, by a gate. This takes you into a walled track, where you should turn right.

Top of Thurlstone

A quick trot along this lane brings you to a T-junction at Top o' th' Town. The town in question is Thurlstone. The village of Thurlstone is first recorded in Domesday in 1086, where it appears as "Turulfestune". Its meaning is "the farmstead (or village) belonging to the man named Thorulf". Unlike a number of place names where the personal name element is unknown except as part of place names, this one is recorded elsewhere and is of Scandinavian origin. At the T-junction go left. Thurlstone proper lies to your right and below. Until the railway reached Penistone in the 1840s, Thurlstone was the bigger village, with an economy based on sheep and the associated spinning and weaving trades. Many of the old weavers cottages still survive. The village also boasts an orchestra and a brass band, both of which are over a hundred years old. Probably the best known "Thurlstonian" was Nicholas Saunderson. Born in 1682, he became blind after contracting smallpox. The story is that he taught himself to read by fingering the incised lettering on gravestones in Penistone churchyard. Quite a feat. What is beyond doubt is that he became sufficiently well-educated to attend University and be awarded the Professorship of Maths at Cambridge.

Ahead you can see Penistone church and the viaduct carrying the railway line to Huddersfield.

Carry on along this lane, ignoring the footpath sign on the left. At this point the track goes sharp right and joins the road. Go right here and descend the road towards Thurlstone, with a very good view to the left. When you reach the T-junction at the bottom of the hill, go left.

Follow the narrow lane, ignoring the tempting stile on the right just before the barn. The lane is tree lined and tarred, though it can't see much traffic at all. The

River Don lies just down the hill to the right. Eventually the river does a great sweep to the north and comes very close to the lane. At this point the tarred road finishes abruptly at a gate cum stile. An obvious path continues ahead through the field, with the fence immediately to the right. On the hillside to the left is a fine example of a nineteenth century chapel, which looks very impressive from this angle. When the farm is reached at the far end of the field there is another gate and stile, which lead into a narrow walled lane. In less than 100 metres this disgorges onto the main road and here you go right.

Bridge End and the drinker's choice

Descend the hill to Bridge End and the junction with the A628, by the garage. Turn right onto the A628 and cross the Don by a fine turnpike bridge. Just beyond the bridge, at the traffic lights, cross the road and go left. There is a tempting choice of pubs here, with the Bridge Inn serving Bass beers and the New Tavern dispensing Theakstons or Youngers. Less than 100 metres from the lights, bear left along Wentworth Road, passing Penistone Motor Spares. Surprisingly, the map shows Wentworth Road as a public footpath, but whilst it is true that it is not a through motor route, it is certainly a road. Pass the bollards which split the street in two and continue ahead, ignoring turnings and paths to left or right. The road is perched above the new housing on the left and there is a good view across to the Huddersfield line viaduct. Soon the road climbs and curves away to the right to a T-junction with the B6462. To the left is the railway bridge carrying the Huddersfield line. To the right is the bridge which carried the former Woodhead railway line to Manchester. Go right and just before the Woodhead line bridge, opposite the Wentworth Arms, (a Mansfield house), go left to reach the station.

21. Rother Valley Country Park

The Route: Bedgrave Mill Visitor Centre, Rother Valley Lake (West bank), Netherthorpe, Meadowgate Lake, County Dike, Wales Bar, Delves Lane, Bedgrave Mill.

Distance: 8.5km (5.3 miles)

Start: Bedgrave Mill Visitor Centre. GR. 424827

Map(s): OS 1:25000 Pathfinder Series No. 744, Aughton and Carlton in Lindrick.

How to get there:

By public transport: There are frequent services to Rother Valley Country Park from Sheffield, Rotherham and North East Derbyshire. Some services come to the Visitor Centre, but there are many others which skirt the perimeter of the park, so the walk could be joined at a number of points.

By car: The country park is signed off the M1 at both the A57 and A616 junctions. Follow the brown/white signs onto the A618, then along the main access road to the car park adjacent to the Bedgrave Mill Visitor Centre. Parking currently costs £1 and the gates close at 8.45pm.

The Walk

Bedgrave Mill

Either before you start the walk or when you get back, go into the Bedgrave Mill Visitor Centre. The country park committee, a joint organisation of local authorities from Derbyshire and South Yorkshire, have done a splendid restoration job on the buildings and the machinery. There is an exhibition showing how the country park was developed from an industrial wasteland, how the river floods have been controlled and the sort of plant and animal life one can expect to find. The mill is in working order and there is an assortment of craft shops in the other buildings. The information centre has details of other walks and activities in the area, including boat hire. There is also a cafe which does a most welcome cup of tea after a walk.

From the visitor centre make your way down to the lake and turn right along the lakeside path. No chance of getting muddy here, the path is tarred. Note on your right the unusual suspension bridge over the River Rother. You will cross the river later on in the walk, but suffice it to say for now that it had the unenviable reputation of being one of Britain's dirtiest rivers. It is reassuring to note that the water in the various lakes does not come from the Rother and that the river itself is now regarded as sufficiently improved to be able to support some fish life.

Visitor Centre, Rother Valley

Continue alongside the Central Lake, avoiding the unwelcome attentions of the scavenging ducks, until you come to the children's playground. Bear left here, on the causeway between the North and Central Lakes. When the walk was being reconnoitred the North Lake was being used by motorised water scooters. Everyone seemed to be thoroughly enjoying themselves, but the racket was tremendous. Continue along the causeway until you come to a T-junction at the far side of the lake. Go left here and pass through a set of double gates which take you onto the west bank track. The Central Lake should now be on your left, though there is some part grown screen planting between you and the water. Killamarsh village and church are in view ahead. On your right is the railway line and the "new" Mosborough housing. The railway is the original North Midland route of the mid 1830s, engineered by George Stephenson. Despite losing its main line status in 1870 and now being used for freight only, it has outlived two later lines along this valley, one of which occupied the area of rough ground between you and the existing line. Mosborough "new" town was designed in the late 1960s to act as an overspill area for Sheffield. The planners envisaged that every household would have a car and that bus use would be minimal. The road system and the housing was designed accordingly. Thankfully, wiser councils prevailed and where a dual three lane motorway was to have been there is now a new tram system.

Child of the lunatic fringe

At the next gate, go right and pass under the railway, then turn left onto the signposted

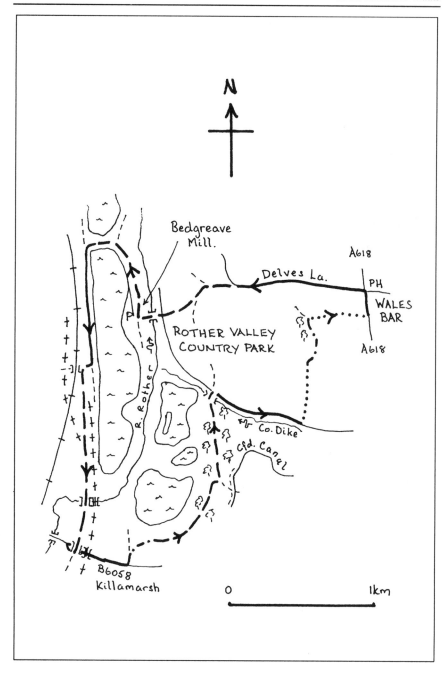

N

Bedgreave
Mill.

A618

Delves La.

PH

WALES
BAR

A618

ROTHER VALLEY
COUNTRY PARK

R. Rother

Co. Dike

Cfd. Canal

B6058
Killamarsh

0   1km

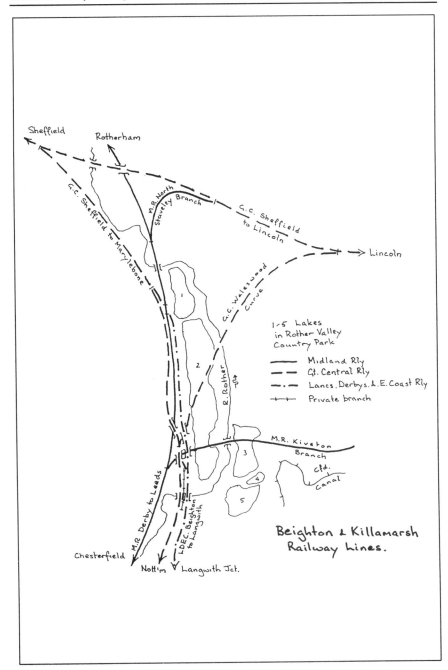

Beighton & Killamarsh
Railway Lines.

trail. This soon betrays its railway origins. It was the end of the so called Sheffield branch of that grandest of all railway projects, the Lancashire Derbyshire and East Coast Railway. It was described by one contemporary railway chairman as "the maddest scheme ever presented to Parliament", and by another railway historian as "the final flowering from the lunatic fringe of railway mania". Needless to say, most of it was never built. It never reached Lancashire, or the East Coast and 90% of the built mileage was outside Derbyshire! Continue along the trail, with the Midland line on your right and the LDEC on your left, until you reach an impressive girder bridge on the right. This carried the third of the valley's railways, the Great Central, over the Midland and off on its route to London Marylebone. The trail slants up to join the GC alignment, which is then followed southwards.

Soon after joining the GC there is a bridge on the left. This bridge carried a Midland Railway branch under the LDEC, through what is now the Central Lake and Meadowgate Lake, en route to Kiveton Park colliery. A glance at the following plan will demonstrate how complex the railway junctions were in this area and how much has changed over the last 30 years.

Carry on along the trail, ignoring the footpath sign on the right and passing over the Midland's Kiveton branch alignment. Where the trail forks, keep right. The left-hand fork was the junction between the GC and the LDEC, installed in 1906 when the two companies merged. In between there is the alignment of a private siding, leading down to the remains of a bridge over the Rother. The trail also crosses the Rother, but on a substantial bridge. To the left is the starkly functional LDEC viaduct. This was designed to be adjusted in the event of mining subsidence, a wise precaution in these parts. Beyond the Rother bridge, the trail is carried on a high embankment which gives good views over the surrounding countryside and the encroaching housing and industry. You are now in Derbyshire, the river being the boundary. Derbyshire have yet to remove the ballast from the trail so the going is quite rough.

Soon another bridge is reached, carrying the trail over the B6058. Go over the bridge and then descend a steep path on the right to reach the road. Here turn right and pass underneath the GC bridge. The road leading off to the right, just past the bridge, was the access to Killamarsh Central station. Despite its small size, Killamarsh once boasted three stations, one on each railway. Now it has none.

Into the Country Park again

Continue on the main road, under the LDEC bridge. For those in need of refreshment, the Midland, (a pub, not a railway) lies on the right. Meals are served at lunchtimes and evenings. Continue past the Midland and past the Killamarsh JAC and I club. Don't ask what the initials stand for, the author has no idea. Just past the club, cross the road and turn left up a narrow lane by the cricket ground. After a short distance bear right at the car park and go left, up the steps onto the embankment which surrounds the southern lakes in the country park. On reaching the top of it, go right and walk along the top, ignoring paths to right and left. The embankment encloses the low lying area of the park and is a flood control measure. Pictures of the floods and their devastating effects are on display in the visitor centre.

Follow the embankment, which curves gently round the southern end of the park, until you are almost heading north. At this point the path suddenly turns right to a gate and a junction of tracks. Go left here, following the signpost for Wales Bar. Notices on your left indicate that this area is part of the nature reserve. Please respect it. At the next junction of paths, go straight on, still following the signs for Wales Bar. (The path off to the right leads up to the Chesterfield Canal).

The track wanders through newish plantations, with glimpses down to the lakes on the left and up to Wales Bar on the hilltop ahead. Soon you reach the main access road to the country park. If you want to cut the walk short and not visit the pub, go left here and follow the road back to the visitor centre. Otherwise, turn right and follow the footway alongside the access road. Ignore the first sign on the left, directing you to Waleswood and carry on along the footway, passing the car pay point. The road is roughly parallelling the course of the canal, just to the right, on the opposite side of the shallow valley of the County Dike. The course of the road must be very close to the alignment of the Midland Railway's Kiveton Park branch, which we met with earlier. Just beyond the pay point is a signpost on the left, by a millstone. Go left here, through the gate and enter fields again, taking care to avoid the ditch. This path may well change in the near future. There were signs posted at strategic points indicating that a golf course was proposed in the area. The alternative route will no doubt be signed. Carry on up the field with the fence on the right and the pub in view on the hilltop.

A Visit to Wales

At the left- and right-hand kink in the fence, go straight on, through the stile ahead. Ignore the stile on the right, which doesn't appear on the map at all. The path now runs through an area of new planting, not shown on the map. Follow the waymarks. The fence does another left and right-hand kink and the waymarks indicate the route straight ahead. However, you should now look out for a stile on the right. This deposits you in a field, across which there is no obvious path. There is however a good waymarker, the pub. The path heads diagonally left across the field, making for a gap in the left-hand hedge. Do not go through the gap but follow the hedge to a stile by a gate. There is a good view back from this point, right over the Rother Valley to Mosborough and beyond.

Carry on alongside the hedge, looking out for convenient gaps through which to dodge if the grazing horses get too frisky. The path ascends to a stile, by a gate and thus emerges onto the main Mansfield Road. Go left if you wish to visit the pub, making use of the footway thoughtfully provided.

Winged connoisseurs needed

From the pub, cross the A618 and go down Delves Lane immediately opposite. It sports a No Through Road sign. As you progress down the lane, the signs of continued coal working become obvious on your right. There are glimpses through the hedge and fence of an enormous opencast pit. The best view into it is at the point where a footpath sign points through the hedge and implies a route across the void. Even if there was such a route, it would only be for the most enthusiastic connoisseur of opencast techniques – and one equipped with wings at that.

The view to the other side of Delves Lane is much better. Continue down Delves Lane, passing the house with the FC 1915 inscription and the coronet. Where the lane goes right, keep straight on, through the gates into the country park again. The route to Bedgrave Mill is signed from this point. The track rises steadily and from the highest point there is an unusual view to the left, to the M1 perched on its embankment where it crosses the line of the Chesterfield Canal. Ignore both the highland cattle and the ladder stile on the right, but continue along the track which soon begins to descend quite sharply. There is a good panorama over the country park from here and no excuse for getting lost from this point on.

Ignoring paths going off to the left, follow the track down to the road and then go over the bridge, noting the regulating gate for controlling the flow of the Rother. Thus you reach the visitor centre again.

22. Sykehouse

The Route: Sykehouse Bridge, New Junction Canal, Kirk Lane Bridge, New Junction Canal, Sykehouse Lock, Sykehouse, Thorseby Hall, Eskholme, Plaice Hills Farm, New Junction Canal, Sykehouse Bridge.

Distance: 6.5km (4 miles)

Start: Sykehouse Bridge Car park. GR. 644175

Map(s): OS 1:25000 Pathfinder Series No. 705 Thorne

How to get there:

By public transport: there is (amazingly) a daily service from Doncaster! Alight at the Old George

By car: Not the easiest place to find by car! From the M18/A614 junction near Thorne, go north on the A614 for about 750 metres, then left at Hangman's Hill, signed to Fishlake and Sykehouse. Go through Fishlake, following the Sykehouse signs and after what seem like an eternity wandering through lanes you will reach Kirk Lane Bridge over the New Junction Canal. Go over the bridge and after about another kilometre turn right at the cross roads. Sykehouse Bridge can be seen ahead. Just before you reach it, there is a lane on the left, not signed. The car park lies about 250 metres along the lane.

The Walk

Serious climbing?

This is an easy, level walk. The greatest ascent is over the stiles. You could be miles from anywhere. Indeed you are miles from anywhere! From the car park, retrace your steps down the lane to the main road and there go left to Sykehouse Bridge. This is not your ordinary hump back bridge over a narrow canal, but a lifting bridge over a wide, barge canal. Until about 1980 it was worked by hand. It is all very impressive, but all too little used. The author was lucky when he reconnoitred this walk, for the bridge was being lifted for a cabin cruiser to pass through. Do not cross the bridge, especially when it is open, but turn right at the canal and proceed along the wide towpath. The canal is the highest thing for miles around and bears obvious witness to the lateness of its construction. It runs straight as a die and is wide enough for Humber barges to use. It was built in the early years of this century, as a link between the South Yorkshire Navigation and the Aire and Calder system. This avoided the devious haul round via Keadby and the tidal Trent, or the less commodious Barnsley Canal. Time was when you could expect to see great trains of coal barges, known as Tom Puddings, plying this waterway, but now its serenity is rarely disturbed.

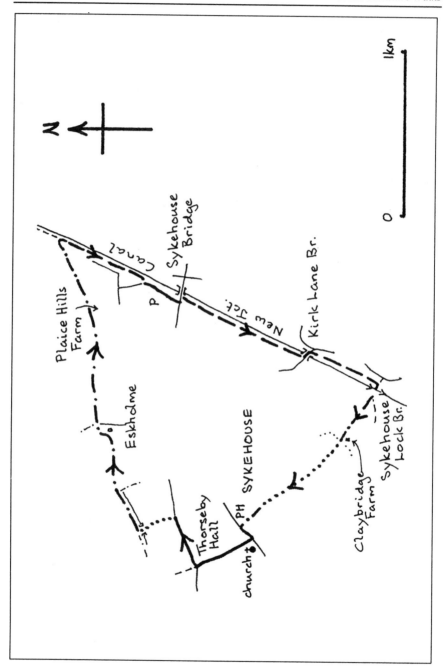

Sykehouse Lock

Along the New Junction

Make your way along the towpath, which is marked out for match fishing. When the author walked this way there were only two fishermen who were calmly sharing the water with a more successful heron. Because the canal is on embankment, the view is quite extensive. The cooling towers of power stations are the most prominent landmarks, but they are miles away, near Doncaster. Nearer is Kirk Lane Bridge, which is soon reached. A gate leads out onto the road, where you should turn left to cross the canal. Once over the bridge, turn right to continue along the towpath. There is another unsigned car park here, obviously designed for those in the know, presumably the fishermen. A further easy stroll takes you to Sykehouse Lock. For those of you who are used to the narrow locks of the Midlands waterways this will be a revelation. It is huge by British standards, though still small by continental reckoning. The cabin cruiser which had been seen earlier, was just locking through when the reconnaissance party arrived. It was dwarfed by the scale of the lock and bobbed and danced on the boiling water that churned into the lock when the paddles were opened. There is something fascinating about watching a boat come through a lock and we spent quite some time here, though the paddles and gates are all mechanised.

Cross the canal again at the lock, either on the now fixed swing bridge, or at the gates. Once over, a gate in the canal fence leads into a lane. Ignore the footpath sign on the left and follow the hedged lane, over a cattle grid and along the driveway to Claybridge Farm. Just before the farm, look out for a yellow waymarker on the wall.

Follow the way it points, round to the right of the house, to a waymarked gate. The only intrusion into an otherwise totally rural landscape is the distant view of the inevitable cooling towers of power stations.

Into Sykehouse through the back garden

From the farm to Sykehouse the path is not distinct underfoot, but there should be no difficulty in route finding. Make your way through the gate and its accompanying quagmire, heading straight across the field to reach a stile in the boundary fence. From this lofty vantage point you will see the spire of Sykehouse church, which forms a useful waymark. Straight on, heading for the church. The map shows a number of field boundaries which normally would be good guides, but some have been removed. The next stile is in the far right-hand corner of the field and is again waymarked. The path then continues alongside the hedge and ditch.

The hedge is obviously of some antiquity as there are fully grown trees in it, including some gnarled oaks. These seem to be favourites of squirrels. We disturbed a number of the grey variety on this stretch. At the end of this field there is an obvious gateway. Too obvious, for this is not your route. The stile you want lies to the right, well-hidden behind a blackthorn bush and an oak tree. This stile drops you neatly into the back "garden" of the Old George, which can now be seen ahead. Make your way along the left-hand side of this field, ignoring the temptation to have a go on the children's play equipment on the right. A gate leads to the rear entrance to the pub and also to the main road, where there is a bus stop. One of the annoying things about bus stops in this area is the lack of timetables. They all have a rotating information "board", but this is more often than not filled with adverts. At best you'll get the route number and the destinations, but the timetable, never.

From the pub, turn left along Broad Lane, towards the church. Sykehouse claims to be the longest village in Yorkshire, but for those used to the compact villages of the Peak District, it scarcely seems to be a village at all. Rather a long disconnected straggle of houses. Originally there were two pubs, a slaughterhouse, blacksmiths, a school, a railway station and a mill. The rot set in with the railway station for despite being equipped to offer a passenger service, no passenger trains ever called and the line is now closed. The place name Sykehouse has a pure Norse derivation, though it was not recorded until the early 15th century. The name means "house by the stream". The Norse word "sik" for stream, occasionally crops up in the North Derbyshire/South Yorkshire, sometimes as in Sykehouse, but at other times as a separate word as part of a river name, e.g. Hipper Sick and Umberley Sick. A corruption of the same word occurs as "sitch" on the Yorkshire Derbyshire boundary.

Below sea level

At the red brick church, turn right, along Chapel Lane. In about 300 metres you pass Thorseby Hall on the right. This is not to be confused with the much grander Thoresby Hall in Nottinghamshire, but it is a large building for this part of the world. Beyond the hall there are deep ditches on either side of the lane, so beware if you have managed to have a jar or two at the Old George. According to the map you are

5 metres above sea level at this point, so a tumble into these ditches would mean that you were below the sea.

A cross roads is reached. Here you go right, along North Lane, which is signed as a bridleway. The lane is hemmed in by a hedge and ditch on either side, so there is no escape if the local cavalry decide to charge. Fortunately there was not much evidence of horses. After about 400 metres, just before the lane bends to the right, there is a footpath sign on the left. Leave the lane at this point, passing through a gap in the hedge and keeping the barn to your right. Follow the hedge up to the point where it does a crafty left and right kink. A stile breaches the hedge and drops you onto a bridge over a ditch. Once over the ditch, bear left to come alongside the hedge and follow it to a waymarked stile in the field corner. A stiff scramble (for this area) takes you from the field, up onto the flood bank, where you turn right. The first thing you will see is of course the chimneys and cooling towers of the nearby power stations. At this distance they look very impressive and even the constant billow of steam and smoke has its attractions when caught by the sun.

Oaks, Alders and Ings

The walk along the flood bank is very pleasant, fringed as it is with oaks and alders. To the left and hidden from view is the River Went, which is the county boundary. Between you and the river are the Old Ings, which are areas of pasture that were subject to regular flooding. To the right is the protected farmland. The floodbank continues for about half a kilometre, until Eskholme Farm is reached. A signpost directs you to the left, alongside a barn. The farm has its quota of yapping dogs, which were mercifully fastened up when we passed this way. Skirt to the left of the barn and so reach a gate. You are still on the flood bank, which here sweeps round the farm buildings. Beyond the gate the path goes to the right, following the fence line. The river is now only one field away but is still not obvious. Two stiles follow in quick succession. These are accompanied by signposts. Go straight on, ignoring the steps down to the right and the path leading away to the left. The route still follows the flood bank, which now becomes an obvious feature again. Horses occupy the field to the right and seem to venture onto the flood bank as well. This explains the monumental stile, which is clearly designed to deter all but the most sophisticated of horses, and most walkers! Thereafter the flood bank path continues as normal, fringed by trees and now accompanied by ditches in which there is a plentiful growth of reeds. This is a marvellous area for bird life in Spring.

Back to Sykehouse Bridge

A further stile leads onto a stretch of bank which has seen some new planting of trees. You are now adjacent to Plaice Hills Farm, seen to the right. To the left across the flat lands of the Went Ings you can see the M62. You can just sense the dull rumble of traffic, largely because there is nothing else making any appreciable noise. Continue along the flood bank to another stile, beyond which the bank appears to end abruptly in a higher embankment. The path tops this rise to reveal the canal again. To the left can be seen the bridge which takes the path over the canal, just by the Went Aqueduct. However, your route lies to the right, along the towpath. Ignore the steps down to the right after about 200 metres. True, these lead to a lane and a car park, but not the one where you were told to leave your car, so don't panic. Continue along the towpath towards Sykehouse Bridge, noting the milestone on the right. About 200 metres before the bridge there is another flight of steps down to the right. These lead off the embankment, across a bridge over a ditch, and so to the lane and the car park where you started your walk.

23. Thorne

The Route: Thorne (Canal Tavern), Wykewell Bridge, Moor's Bridge, Stainforth and Keadby Canal, Maud's Bridge, Crook o' Moor Bridge, Dirtness Grove Fm., Godknow Bridge, Crowle Bridge, Crowle Wharf, Crowle station.

Distance: 13.75km (8.5 miles)

Start: The Canal Tavern in Thorne. Dry parking underneath the arches of the new(ish) road bridge GR 687130. The access to the Canal Tavern lies immediately north of the A614 canal bridge. It is a public road but the turn is very awkward and easily misjudged. The author speaks from experience!

Map(s): OS 1:25000 Pathfinder Series No. 705 Thorne

How to get there:

By public transport: Thorne boasts two railway stations with daily trains from Sheffield, Doncaster and Hull (Thorne North), or Grimsby (Thorne South). To get to the starting point, either station will do. Note that the return from Crowle will land you at Thorne South.

By car: from junctions 5 or 6 on the M18, follow the signs to Thorne. From Junction 5 you approach from the south and cross the canal before turning left to the start. From Junction 6 you follow the A614 until just before the canal bridge. The pub and the start lie down the lane to the right, parallel to the main road.

The Walk

Thorne

Surprisingly, the Thorne place name means exactly what you would expect, in other words "thorn tree". This particular shrub was first recorded in 1086, but it is unlikely that the original version has survived! The church has some Norman work, but the tower and chapels are 13th to 15th century. Despite this antiquity, the landscape of the area owes much more to the Dutch engineer, Vermuyden, who initiated a drainage scheme for the marshes in the 17th century. The success of this led to the granting of Thorne's market charter in 1658. The engineers and investors who were involved in the drainage works made considerable fortunes in some cases, though the erstwhile inhabitants were none too pleased by the changes. Despite the drainage, the main means of transport until the railway came in the 1850s, was water. For beer devotees, Thorne is famous for Darley's Ales, taken over first by Wards of Sheffield and then by Vaux. Sadly the brewery closed in 1987. New industry came to the area in the early part of this century with the sinking of Thorne Colliery at Moorends. With a shaft depth of almost 1000 metres it was one of the deepest pits in the country.

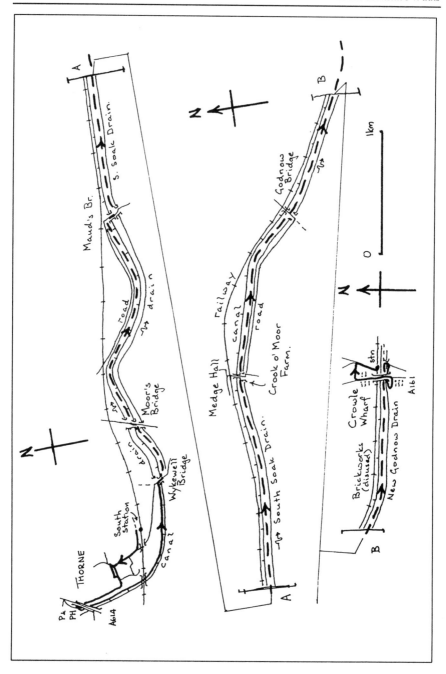

Wykewell Bridge

First bridge of many

Go to the canal bank and turn left along the towpath, passing under the A614 bridge. Follow the canal southwards, with the houses of Thorne on your left. The towpath soon passes under the railway bridge carrying the line from Doncaster, through Thorne South station to Scunthorpe and Grimsby.

Just beyond the railway bridge, the canal swings to the left and soon the lifting bridge at Wykewell End comes into view. This is an impressive structure, though only carrying a minor road. When you reach the bridge, go across and then left, picking up the towpath again. The whole of the walk from now on is hemmed in by water. Deep and wide ditches run parallel with the canal. They are so big that they would class as canals themselves anywhere else in the country. Continue along the towpath, which doesn't see much towing nowadays, nor many walkers, but it does accommodate fishermen in hordes at times, if the numbers are anything to go by.

Soon the next bridge is reached. This is Moor's Bridge. Who was Moor and why did he want a bridge in this out of the way spot? Moor's Bridge is a swing bridge quite unlike the lifting bridge at Wykewell. Cross the bridge and go right, passing the capstan that serves to open the bridge when needed. In the entire journey the author and his companion never encountered a moving boat at all. As you cross the bridge note the level crossing ahead. The railway was built as cheaply as possible and bridges were avoided. As the walk continues you will see some real period pieces of railway crossing architecture, though how much longer they can survive is open to question.

Two! Six! Heave!

When the line was built in 1858, it ran closely parallel to the canal, so that no Act of Parliament was required. This was typical of the railway company which built the line, the South Yorkshire Railway. Of course, the route has been altered since. One of the strangest tales told about this company concerns the inaugural train from Doncaster to Thorne. This was carrying the Inspecting Officer. When the train reached the terminus at Thorne, it was found that there were no facilities to turn the engine or to allow it to get to the other end of the train. Whilst the Inspector was being treated to a "cold collation" – Victorian jargon for an almighty binge, the navvies lifted the engine off the rails, turned it round and carried it to the other end of the train before setting it on the rails again. It is said that the Inspector never noticed, but gave approval for services to begin.

Splendid isolation

There is a strong feeling of isolation walking along this towpath. The canal is slightly above the level of the surrounding land so you get a commanding view. This is the nearest you'll come to a ridge walk in this part of South Yorkshire. To the left you can see the headgear of Moorend colliery, with the power stations beyond. To the right the land seems to stretch interminably flat. Soon the railway closes in from the left and there is another level crossing. The canal takes a bend to the right, leaving the railway to its own devices. The road which came over the railway at Moor Edges crossing now parallels the canal on the left, but separated from it by a deep ditch.

Canal and road sweep to the left beyond Orchards Farm. To the right there is a thin belt of trees, quite an unusual feature alongside this canal, but a welcome wind break. Road, railway and canal now begin to converge again as Maud's Bridge nears. The going becomes quite rough and it is better to leave the canal bank and descend to the left, nearer to the drain, where there is a reasonable track. This soon rises to rejoin the towpath at Maud's Bridge. The map shows a siding from the railway at this point but it has long since been lifted. Maud's Bridge is another swinging variety. Cross the bridge and go left, through a stile and gate to regain the towpath. The canal is now accompanied by the North and South Soak Drains and by the railway. For two kilometres the two drains, the canal and the railway run straight as a die, through a wide, flat landscape, singularly devoid of human habitation. The mirage of hills away to the left turns out to be a view of the Isle of Axholme, but unusually, from this point you can see both ends of the walk!

A series of old brick bridges span the South Soak Drain and when we reconnoitred the walk there was considerable dredging work going on and a new heightened flood bank was under construction. Apart from the regular passage of trains, this was the only sign of activity between the two ends of the walk. Splendid isolation!

Period pieces

The drains, rails and canal bend slightly to the left as Crook o' Moor Bridge is approached. Here again there is a swing bridge and a level crossing with a fine wooden signal box of pre 1923 vintage. This is Medge Hall Crossing. Again the map shows a siding running parallel to the canal, but it has gone. Don't cross the bridge this time, except to admire the signal box. Instead, continue ahead on the south side of the canal, through a stile by a gate. The railway leaves the canalside, taking a sweeping curve away to the north. The two drains and now a minor road, still keep company with the canal. About half a kilometre from Godknow Bridge, the railway rejoins and here we met two fishermen, giving up the unequal struggle against the gale force winds which were whipping the canal up into metre high waves.

At Godknow Bridge there is another level crossing. The road to the left leads directly to the flesh pots of Crowle, which can be seen in the distance. Puritans will continue straight ahead, through the stile and onto the towpath again. About a mile ahead you see the chimney of the former Crowle Brick works, now disused. A useful but disconcerting marker as it never seems to get any nearer, especially if there is an east wind blowing. For reasons that are not immediately apparent there is a gate and stile part way along this stretch of path. Some wind blasted soul has seen fit to plant a strip of trees along the south side of the canal, but it will be some time before they offer any shelter. The canal bends to the left, closely parallelling the railway line.

My life's work

Now the "new" bridge carrying the A161 over the canal, can be seen ahead. The author has a great affection for this bridge. In his first job, for Lindsey County Council he had to undertake the economic justification before the bridge could be constructed. Part of this work involved driving up and down along the old road to assess speeds and traffic flows. The constant jarring as the car bumped across the old swing bridge and the adjacent level crossing had to be experienced to be believed. The car, an old Morris Minor, gave up the ghost the following week!

As the new bridge comes nearer, it becomes clear that the author was too successful in his work, for the old bridge has gone completely. Go under the new bridge and at the site of the old bridge, go right, crossing the New Godknow Drain on a bridge which thankfully still survives. Then turn right and pass underneath the road bridge again, to reach a flight of steps on the left. These take you up onto the road, where you turn left. As this is the highest point for miles around, there is a good view from here. Carry on along the road, passing back over the Godknow Drain, then the canal and finally the railway. The station can be seen just to the right, but unfortunately, there's no direct means of access, unless you fancy a jump. This is not advised, so carry on until you reach the junction which is signposted to the station. Go right here and descend to join the former main road, close to the New Trent pub. Go right and walk 200 metres to the station, passing the old Wharf buildings on the left. Trains for Thorne go from the platform nearest the canal, so you have to cross the lines. Take great care, especially if you are in a hurry.

Not quite finished!

On arrival back at Thorne South station walk down the station approach to the main road and turn right. Take the second turning on the left and follow this road round, until it runs parallel to the canal. It is not a through route for motor vehicles, but on foot you by-pass the bollards and go under the bridge carrying the A614 over the canal and so reach the Canal Tavern and your starting point again.

24. Thurnscoe

The Route: Thurnscoe railway station, Stotfold Rd, Frickley Beck, Frickley Park, Moorhouse Common, Moorhouse Grange, Old Street, Hooton Pagnell, Watchley Lane, Watchley Crag, Stotfold Farm, Thurnscoe East, Thurnscoe.

Distance: 14.5km (9 miles)

Start: Thurnscoe railway station. GR 459056

Map(s): OS 1:25000 Pathfinder Series No. 716 Doncaster and Dearne

How to get there:

By public transport: there is a daily train service from Sheffield, Wakefield and Leeds to Thurnscoe, plus daily buses to Doncaster and Barnsley.

By car: The A635 Dearne link road passes just to the south of Thurnscoe and is accessible from Doncaster or from Barnsley. Thurnscoe is signed off this road and the station car park is on the B6414

The Walk

Chop Suey and Goldfinches

Nobody would describe Thurscoe as a picturesque rural idyll. It is a mining town that has lost its mine, and it shows. For all that, it has character and is an older settlement than the buildings would suggest. The main rise in population took place in the 19th century when the local collieries were sunk. Closure came in the 1980s with all the economic and social effects that one might expect.

From the station car park, go right, along the main street, passing the curious little shop with the roof that seems to be made of concrete thatch, before plunging underneath the railway line. About 100 metres beyond the bridge, just by the Chop Suey House, go right, on what is shown on the map as a bridleway, but is in fact a tarred road. This soon bends to the right and finishes alongside the railway. The path continues to the left, tight between the railway on the right and the houses on the left. This stretch is notable for the number of yapping dogs. Nevertheless, in this unlikely spot, we saw a goldfinch, busily feeding in the hawthorns that fringe the railway.

The path closely follows the railway, though other tracks go off to the left. After about 400 metres, close to a stone gatepost, you come to a T-junction with a track. Turn right here and cross over the railway bridge, noting the fine array of graffiti and bemoaning the lack of original thought behind the sprayed comments. Turn left just beyond the bridge and continue alongside the railway, which here is in deep cutting. Note how the houses on your right, seem to curve away from the railway. This is due to the fact that between the houses and your path, there used to be another railway line, but this has vanished without trace. This was the late lamented Hull and

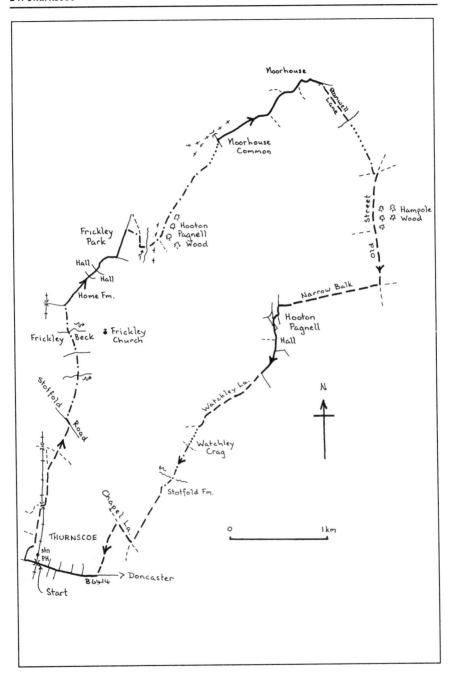

Barnsley Railway, which in better organised countries would never have been built in the first place.

View to Hooton Pagnell and Frickley

After a further 400 metres the track forks again. The path continuing alongside the railway is not shown on the map, but obviously sees regular use. Not by you though, for you should bear right and cross the rough field to reach a cross "roads" with an attendant signpost. Go straight on here and so leave the "urban countryside" of Thurnscoe behind. The scene is now wholly rural. The track is fringed with an unkempt blackthorn hedge, over which, to the right, can be seen Hooton Pagnell Hall, perched on top of the hill. You will pass this later but the view of the hall from this lane is the best you will get. The spire of Frickley church can be seen ahead. This is a curious church, miles from any sizeable village and completely isolated in a field some 200 metres from the nearest road.

Continuing along the track you soon reach a T-junction with Stotfold Road and here you go left. Walk along Stotfold Road for about 100 metres until you reach a hedge on the right. The map shows a bridleway running along the right-hand side of this hedge, but this doesn't happen in practice. Instead the bridleway runs down the left-hand side of the hedge. This is shown on the map as a black dotted line. However, the local highway authority obviously believe that the used line is the correct one, for it is waymarked. Continue down the field to reach a stream. This is crossed by a bridge made of old railway sleepers. Here the path swings first right then left, before resuming its course alongside a hedge until it reaches a road by a footpath sign. The walk can be cut short at this point by turning right, along the road. In a little over 2 km you will reach Hooton Pagnell, where you will pick up the route description again. 400 metres to the right along this road is the track down to Frickley church, which is worth a visit if you have time.

Male chauvinism

For those who are continuing, go across the road and carry straight on with the hedge to the right. Frickley church can now be clearly seen to the right. The path curves gently to the left, still following the hedge, down to the bridge over Frickley Beck. The bridge is guarded by a stile which was slippery when the author reconnoitred this walk. Either that or the John Smiths was beginning to take its toll on his balance. Beyond the stream the path bears right, following the hedge up the field. The local farmer was having some trouble in persuading his cows to come in for the milking when we passed by. There was some good natured banter about the difficulty of getting the female of whatever species to do what was wanted, when required. Fortunately for the farmer, he was not within striking distance of the more militant femanist members of the reconnaissance party. A stile at the top of the field leads into a lane, where you go right, to pass Frickley Home Farm.

Ha, Ha! Frickley Hall

Continue along the lane which soon enters the woodland of Frickley Park. Continue straight ahead at the crossing of tracks, noting what the map describes as Frickley

Hall to the left. A short distance further on the track negotiates a cattle grid, which is bypassed to the left. The track then swings right and passes in front of an imposing building, which must be the real Frickley Hall, to the right. The formal gardens are separated from the track by the classic landscape design feature of a "Ha-Ha". This consists of a ditch with a wall on one side. It is designed to keep cattle out of the gardens of the "big" house, whilst allowing the owners to have an uninterrupted view, through the gardens to open fields.

At the junction of lanes, just beyond the house, go left. The route is waymarked. Note the curious stone in the field on the left. There was speculation about its origin ranging from an ancient cross base, to a rubbing post for cattle. Continue down the lane in totally rural surroundings towards the belt of trees. The lane passes through a gap in the trees to reveal a surprising site, for the rural idyll is abruptly swept away by the presence of the spoil heaps and buildings of Frickley Colliery. Quite a shock and obviously the reason why the owners of Frickley Hall planted the belt of trees which effectively closed off their view.

Over Frickley Beck again

Just beyond the trees, there is a gateway on the right and a waymarked stile. Go right here and follow the indistinct path alongside the trees until a track joins from the left. The map indicates that the path should bear right at this point and cut diagonally across the field. However, there is a waymark on the big ash tree, which indicates that you should turn right and follow the track towards the farm. When you reach the farm gate, there is another waymark pointing left, down the edge of the field, alongside the wall. In this manner you will reach a small bridge over Frickley Beck, with its fringe of trees. Cross the stream into the field beyond and bear left along a barely discernible path. When the path reaches the strip of trees it becomes more obvious and there is a waymark. The strip of trees is the course of the old Hull and Barnsley Railway, though it is hard to believe that now. Indiscernibly, the railway land merges with the scrub surrounding Hooton Pagnell Wood and the path splits. Follow the left-hand, waymarked path. The map shows a narrow field between the wood and the railway, but this is now getting very overgrown and will soon be a wood. The path weaves its way through the scrub, with a fence to the right. An occasional waymark gives some sense of security through the jungle and eventually you emerge into a more open area, though still with the wood to your right.

Answers on a postcard

When you reach the end of the wood, the path continues straight ahead across the field. It is waymarked and distinct underfoot. In a short distance there are some curious structures on the left with the tops of ladders sticking out of them. They are not shown on the map and there was some speculation as to their purpose. Any sensible ideas on a postcard please, to the author. The path has been closely parallelling the railway alignment, which here in the fields has virtually been ploughed out of existence. Continue straight ahead, now with a hedge to your right, until a gateway is reached. Beyond the gateway is a bridge, which was well-disguised and slippery when the author attempted to cross it, so take care. Away to the left, contractors were in the throws of demolishing the colliery buildings, so by the time this book is printed the scene will be very different. The large spoil heap is likely to remain however. Another gateway follows and the path runs alongside a ditch and hedge on the right to reach a third gate. Again this is accompanied by a bridge and once through you are on the edge of a large open field. The waymarker isn't much use here, but you should bear left across the field, making for the right-hand end of the red brick house. Here a gateway leads out onto Elmsall Lane. The red brick house has unmistakeable railway origins and was once the station building for South Elmsall station. Here there was a junction of lines, but all have now gone.

A contrast in railways

At the road go left and then immediately right, along Moorhouse Lane. The former railway is just to the left, now appearing as an overgrown embankment. Walk along Moorhouse Lane, which doesn't see a great deal of traffic. Ignore the footpath sign on the right and carry on, passing the very attractive garden on the left. For those with railway interests, there is now a view to the left to the East Coast Main Line, recently electrified. The regular and rapid passage of trains on this route is in sharp contrast to the now derelict remains of the Hull and Barnsley line.

Moorhouse Grange is soon reached and here there is a large equestrian centre. Ignore the footpath sign on the right and continue along the road. taking care round the bend by Gap Farm, as there is no footway. Beyond the farm the road begins to climb and soon a track forks off to the right. This is your route and it is marked with a footpath sign. This has obviously been more than a mere path, for it is a pleasant hedged lane. The lane climbs quite sharply, towards the strip of trees on the skyline. At the trees the gradient eases and the lane soon reaches a road.

Cross the road and survey the route ahead. The lane has ceased and there is a large field in front. The path heads slightly to the right, making for the line of trees and the white posts which you will see in mid field. Though these are useful markers, they appear to be nothing at all to do with the path. When you reach the trees, the path continues ahead, now with a hedge to the left. Field boundaries shown on the map have been removed with great thoroughness here. It is not until the unmistakable alignment of Long Baulk is reached that the map and the ground really correspond. The arrangement of fields, lane and boundary hedges from hereon is a fossilisation of the medieval strip farming.

Of Baulks, long, broad and narrow

At Long Baulk, a green track, go left for about 100 metres until a T-junction is reached with Old Street. Despite the name, this is a lovely green lane, fringed with trees and bushes, a real delight. The name would seem to indicate a possible Roman origin. Walk along Old Street, savouring its timeless quality and "away from it all" feeling. We met a party gathering sloes, "for gin". There were plenty of sloes and now I suspect there may be one or two headaches in Hooton Pagnell. Soon the lane runs alongside Hampole Wood on the left and at the southern end of the wood there is a T-junction. Broad Baulk runs away to the right, but your route carries straight on along Old Street, here called Lound Lane. This rises steadily towards Lound Hill, which can be seen ahead. A further 400 metres or so of this lovely green lane follows, until a cross roads is reached. Here there is a veritable plethora of signs, footpath, bridleway and the much rarer by-way. The route of this walk lies to the right, along Narrow Baulk, but to the left lies the miserably named Rat Hall. A canine companion on our reconnoitre proved the truth of this name by finding and consuming a rat during our traverse of Lound Lane. I am happy to say that the dog suffered no apparent ill effects, but it is not the sort of food I would advocate for starving walkers.

Go along Narrow Baulk, which despite the name would accommodate a tractor. Like Lound Lane this too is a green lane, fringed with hedges and trees. It runs almost dead straight for about a kilometre, until a T-junction is reached with Back Lane, close to a half timbered house. You are now on the edge of the village of Hooton Pagnell. Go left here and then almost at once turn right through the signposted gateway. The church can be seen to the left. This is a Norman foundation though with much later embellishment, including an 18th century pulpit of unusual design. The narrow lane soon emerges onto the village main street almost opposite the beautifully-preserved Pinfold.

Hooton Pagnell – a flawed idyll

Unlike Thurnscoe, Hooton Pagnell is a picture postcard of a village, but it lacks one feature to make it completely idyllic. It has no pub! So far as the villagers are concerned this unmitigated disaster is redeemed by the the Hooton Pagnell Club. This occupies a fine Mock Tudor (1903) building on the main street and serves John Smiths Beers. Alas, you have to be members to drink here, or a bona-fide guest of a member who will sign you in. As the reconnaissance party were neither, there was no room for us at the Club, though we were allowed to use the car park.

Hooton inevitably turns up first in the Domesday Book, but the Pagnell part of the name derives from the Norman Lords of the Manor, the de Pagnels. The manor has passed through a number of hands since then, but the village name has not changed. The present owners, the Warde-Norburys, keep the estate in a pristine condition that deserves commendation.

The Pinfold and the 13th century butter cross are each worth a look, as is the fine view across the valley. Then turn left, along the main street and shake the dust of Hooton Pagnell off your feet for the final stretch back to Thurnscoe. As you head through the village you pass the Hall which you saw earlier, on your left. At the main gate is a mounting block for prospective horse riders. The Hall is of medieval vintage and the gateway is 14th century. Carry on along the main road to the junction with Butt Lane, ignoring the footpath sign to the right. Straight on at the junction, still on the main road, passing the cricket ground on the left. After about 400 metres, the road veers left, but a track continues ahead. This is your route.

Watchley Crags

This track has the name Watchley Lane and it is aptly called, for there is a grand view to the right. That largest of all marker stones, the television tower at Emley Moor, is clearly visible and the Dearne valley stretches away for miles. Watchley Lane is perched on the edge of a small scarp, but the view is often obscured by trees. The map shows these as plantations so their presence is presumably deliberate. Notice the peculiar inverted triangular water tower. It looks decidedly unsafe. Soon the track has trees on both sides. This is Little Watchley.

As you emerge from the trees, the track begins to dip to the right, down the slope. About 100 metres beyond the trees, the track bears right. Leave the track at this point and head straight across the field, just clearing the corner of the wood on your right and making for the middle of the belt of trees on the opposite side of the field. There is no obvious path in the field, but, if your navigation has proved correct you should find a distinct path when you reach the trees. This leads steeply down what is known as Watchley Crag – there are some rocks evident, until a track is reached. This of course is the track you left a few moments ago.

Cross the track and continue along the path which soon emerges into fields again. Here at least there is no difficulty, for the path follows the hedge and ditch on the right. The misshaped tower on the sky line is Hoober Stand, visited by another of these walks and seen on many more.

View over the Dearne Valley

At the end of the field there is a stile by an old willow tree. A culvert takes you safely over the stream and now Stotfold Farm can be seen ahead. Go up the track with a fence to your left, taking care to duck underneath the electric fence which was strung across the path near the farm. Another stile leads out onto a track and the farm is bypassed to the left. Again there are views over the Dearne Valley, particularly to Dearne itself and Goldthorpe. The gaunt remains of colliery headgear can now be seen ahead, mute reminders of a vanished industry. Follow the track down to the T-junction with Chapel Lane.

Duck! Flying Lead

You have left the rural idyll behind. This is very much urban fringe countryside, with the inevitable rubbish dump. Turn right along Chapel Lane and continue along this track until you reach a footpath sign on the left, just by the playing fields. This sign is most unusual. It requests that you don't use firearms! Unfortunately this order seems to have resulted in the sign being peppered with gunshots. If in doubt keep your head down and pass by quickly. Go left at the sign, into Thurnscoe Community Park. Keep to the left-hand side of the field to join a tarred track, which turns first left, then right before running down between the houses on the left and the pond on the right. A stile, the last vestige of a rural path, leads onto the main road, just opposite the former colliery site. Turn right here and make your way along the main road, passing the Thurnscoe Business Park on Phoenix Lane, an appropriate name and the best of luck. A final 500 metres or so along the road brings you to The Station and the end of the walk.

25. Tickhill

The Route: Tickhill, Broadheads, Wellingley Lane, Dadsley Well Bridge, Stancil Lane, Stancil, Dadsley Well Stream, Hopyard Lane, Common Lane, Tollbar Bridge, Tickhill Castle, Tickhill.

Distance: 10km (6.2 miles)

Start: Tickhill village car park. GR 591933

Map(s): OS 1:25000 Pathfinder Series Nos. 727 Rotherham and 728 Harworth.

How to get there:

By public transport: Daily bus services from Doncaster, Maltby and Rotherham. Alight near the Butter Cross in the centre of the village.

By car: The A1 passes perilously close to Tickhill, but there is no access from it. Instead you should approach by either the A60 or the A631. These meet in the centre of the village. The car park is signed off the A60 and lies very close to the centre of the village but hidden from the main road, just to the north of the church.

The Walk

Tickhill

From the car park, make your way through St Mary's Court with its little shops, under the archway, to emerge on the main road near the Butter Cross. This was erected in 1777 at the junction of the three routes into the village. The market would have been held around it. Go left at the main road and walk up this wide and busy street, passing the Three Crowns (Tetleys) and the Royal Oak (Whitbread) as you go. Notice that many of the older buildings are constructed with limestone, which is the indigenous building material of the area. The village is ancient, being recorded in Domesday. There are two possible derivations of the place name. Tickhill can either be translated as "the hill of a man called Tica", or "the hill where goats are kept". In either case the source is Old English.

At the end of the houses on the right-hand side of the road, there is a footpath sign. Time was when this would have been of use to you, but some kind soul has built the A1(M) across the line of the path, so it now goes nowhere. You can see the A1 across the fields to the right and you will shortly make a closer acquaintance with it.

At the point where Dadesley Road trails in from the left, keep straight on along the main A60, which fortunately has a footway. About 150 metres beyond Dadesley Road you reach another road junction. Cross the A60 with care and go right, along the narrow lane, signed to Stancil and Wellingley. This is Wellingley Lane. Go past

Tickhill church

the Tickhill nameplate, nicely secured on a stone plinth, and continue along the lane, making for the A1(M). The fields on either side are large and open, with no hedges. To the right, and looking for all the world like the tower of a great cathedral, you can see the modern headgear of Harworth colliery.

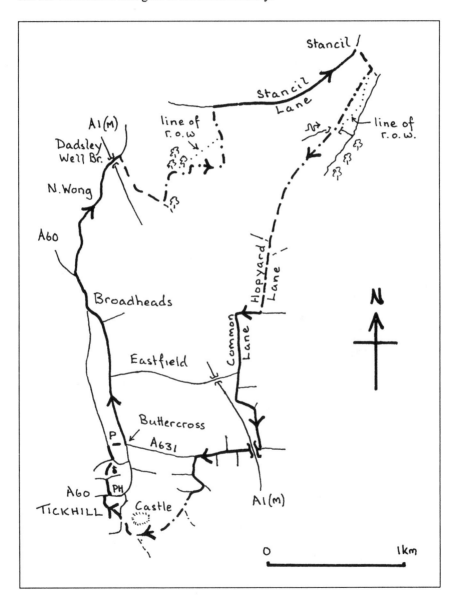

A vanished footpath and a modern motorway

Just past the large oak tree on the left-hand side of the road, the lane swings left. The map shows a footpath leading away to the right here, but although there is a semblance of a field boundary, there is no sign that anyone has walked the route. Nor is there a footpath sign. The more perceptive among you will realise that the route of the path is cut by the A1(M) and there is no apparent means of crossing. Keep on the lane, with a view left to the headgear of Maltby colliery, poking up above the trees. The road climbs and swings right to go over the A1(M). From here there is a good view back towards Tickhill, with the church tower being very prominent.

Cross the A1(M) by the bridge and almost at once go right, following the signed track. The track is separated from the motorway by a belt of trees, but there is still the incessant rumble of traffic. After about 300 metres the track swings left. It is at this point where the footpath referred to in the previous paragraph, should have emerged. It doesn't, so you were right. Another 300 metres and the track ends abruptly by a couple of oak trees.

Go left here and follow a very indistinct path along a bank between two fields, heading for the left-hand side of the coppice. Continue along the bank, where it kinks to the right and in this manner you reach an area of scrub, which extends beyond the coppice proper.

Devious doings in deep ditches

The map indicates that the path bears left at this point, roughly following the boundary of the wood. The footprints on the ground and the density of the scrub indicate otherwise. The walked route skirts the edge of the scrub until a ditch is reached. This is particularly steep-sided and deep and there is no bridge at this point. The author and his companion made a gallant effort to get to the other side and succeeded, only to find that there was no path through this field either and no way out at the other side. The field is bounded on all sides by ditches and what appears to be a waymark post turns out to be a water main sign. Again there is evidence that users of this route do not even attempt to cross the first ditch, but turn right and follow the field edge, turning left at the end. Follow the ditch and boundary, then head along a track towards a large oak tree. This route will shortly become the right of way.

Oh! Blessed tarmac!

Wadsworth village can be seen ahead and to the left, but of more interest is the proximity of Stancil Lane. This is marked by a footpath sign post and the security of a tarmac road is very real after the mud and ditches.

Go right at the lane and bowl merrily along, with your feet getting lighter with every stride as the accumulated mud drops off. Stancil Farm can soon be seen ahead, whilst to the left is the headgear of Rossington Colliery. The surrounding fields are unbelievably stony, with masses of round pebbles.

Go past the Nissen hut type barn on the right. At the end of the barn, just before the farm, the footpath goes off to the right. It does a left and right zigzag to come into a narrow fenced track across the fields, heading for Broomhills Wood. After about 200 metres there are stiles and footpath signs on both sides. Your route is to the right.

An obvious path makes a bee-line across the field towards the tower of Tickhill church. The path coincides with the waymark at the stile, but not with the map. This shows the route running diagonally left to reach the stream then cutting back across the field. There is no evidence that anyone does this. At the far side of the field there is a stile and then a culvert over the Dadsley Well Stream. Another stile follows at once and you are back into fields again. Here the obvious course is to follow the bank of the stream on the right, especially as this seems to be the driest part of the field. However, this is not the route of the path. The right of way cuts diagonally across the field, heading for the fence corner just to the right of the church tower. Hesley Hall can be seen away to the left through the trees.

Along Hopyard Lane

At the fence corner there is a stile which takes you onto an obvious track, with a deep ditch on the left. Progress is now quite brisk, until you reach what can only be described as a stockade. The path is signed at this point and kinks to the left and then to the right, before resuming its course, between ditches and hedges. You are now on Hopyard Lane, though the change in status from footpath to unclassified county highway is scarcely obvious. Pass the footpath sign on the left and continue along the lane. About 300 metres from the stockade there is a gate across the lane. This has to be negotiated as best you may, avoiding an undignified fall into one of the flanking ditches. The lane continues beyond the gate and soon reaches a T-junction. At the junction go right, along another rough track. This is Common Lane, which formed the access from Tickhill village to Tickhill Low Common. Common Lane soon swings to the left and begins to draw steadily nearer to the A1. The roofs of Tickhill village can be seen beyond the motorway. After about 200 metres the lane begins to rise and change character. This section was rebuilt in order to provide an access over the motorway to the village. On the crest of the rise there is a junction. For a quick trot back into Tickhill you could go right here, but the walk carries straight on.

Beyond the junction the lane is tarred and descends to true ground level again. The A1 draws ever nearer, but just when you think that you have been misled and are going to have to walk along the hard shoulder, the lane swings left. The "works" shown on the map turns out to be the local sewage works, but whilst these might not be to everyone's liking, there was certainly a wide variety of bird life in the vicinity. We watched the antics of a flock of Long Tailed Tits for quite some time.

Tickhill's East "Gate"

Continue along the lane for a further 300 metres until you reach the A631 at Tollbar Bridge. The old tollbar cottage is still there on your left, but is now in a sorry state. The bridge in question is presumably the little culvert over the stream and not the massive structure carrying the A1(M) over the A631. Turn right along the main road and pass under the motorway. The bridge serves as a very effective gateway into Tickhill village. The church is now in view ahead and if time presses, or you've had enough, the car can be reached quickly by proceeding straight on, to the centre of the village at the Butter Cross. If you are determined to complete the walk, carry on along the A631 until you reach the third turning on the left. This should be Lumley Drive. If it isn't, either you have miscounted or the author has. Maths was never his strong point but he can read, so rely on the street name.

Circumnavigation of Tickhill Castle

Go down Lumley Drive, ignoring the first turn on the right to Lancaster Crescent. The street names give the clue that this is a modern housing estate. At the second Lancaster Crescent turn, go right and after about 150 metres you should see a footpath sign on the left. This takes you down between the houses to a gate and stile into open fields again. Once in the field the path skirts to the left of the barn, then goes right, alongside the ditch. The remains of Tickhill castle are now in view to the right, a large grassy mound surrounded by trees and crumbling walls. This was one of the ruins that a certain well-known Protector knocked about a bit, presumably because the inhabitants flew the wrong flag from the tower.

The path reaches a multi armed footpath sign by a bridge. Go over the bridge and follow the well-trodden path alongside the ditch and field boundary. This skirts the southern perimeter of the castle, but the trees screen most of the view, even in winter. At the end of the field there is a kissing gate and another multi armed footpath sign. Go right here, passing over the stream on a brick bridge. The path immediately widens to become a muddy track through a farmstead. Still there is no good view of the castle. After a short distance the castle entrance is reached on the right. It is possible to go into the grounds at certain times to view the remains; the notice board gives details.

Return to Tickhill

The track now swings left to join Castlegate Lane, just by the millpond. This is a delightful spot. Turn right here, along Castlegate, passing the former main gateway to the castle on your right. Where the road forks, go left, along Dam Road, still alongside the pond. At Rowlands Bridge, go left briefly for a charming view across the pond to the castle. Retrace your steps to the junction with Dam Road and now go straight on to reach the main A60. Turn right at the main road. The Carpenters' Arms lies a short distance along the A60, just after Church Lane. To return to the car park, either go along Church Lane and through the churchyard, or follow the main road round past the Millstone pub towards the Butter Cross, before turning left through St Mary's Court. If you pass through the churchyard, be sure to pay a visit to the church. Surely this is one of the finest medieval churches in South Yorkshire and certainly the best encountered on any of these walks. Tickhill church is dedicated to St Mary and built in the richly carved Perpendicular style. Its spire is a landmark for miles and it is illuminated at night. Unusually, the bells of St Marys, play a different tune each day. Reputedly, the Saturday version is "Home Sweet Home". Well worth a visit – St Marys, not home.

26. Tinsley (Meadowhall)

The Route: Tinsley (Meadowhall), Sheffield Canal towpath, Sheffield canal basin, The Alexandra Hotel, Exchange St, Commercial Street.

Distance: 7.5km (4.7 miles)

Start: Meadowhall Shopping Complex. Use the car park for the tram terminus and railway station.

Map(s): The A to Z of Sheffield is the only really useful map for this walk, but make sure you get an up to date version. Much has altered in the Tinsley and Attercliffe area in the last few years.

How to get there:

By public transport: Frequent services by bus train and tram from all parts of Sheffield and Rotherham (and from many other parts of the kingdom as well). *By car:* Given the amount and scope of public transport, it seems almost criminal to tell you how to get there by car. However, there are likely to be some renegades who insist on using this form of transport so the instructions are to pick up the innumerable signs for Meadowhall and follow them to the Shopping Complex. There, do not go into the main car park entrance, but skirt round to the right, (following the tram lines and overshadowed by Tinsley M1 viaduct), to find a parking space somewhere near the tram terminus and railway station.

The Walk

Turn away from Mammon

You start at the Meadowhall shopping complex, a singularly unusual place to begin any walk. You will get some strange looks as you make your way in the opposite direction to the crowds trying to get into the centre. From the tram terminus/railway/bus station, make your way round the perimeter of the complex, following the dual carriageway and the tram lines (there is a footway as well so you needn't feel too intimidated). Where the trams veer away to the left there is a tram stop and the canal is just beyond. Unfortunately, the stop was designed for people visiting Meadowhall, so there is no access to the towpath at this point. A bridge is proposed here, but there is some dispute about the design at present. Why one needs a bridge at all to cross a tramway and a very rarely used bit of railway, is beyond me. A level crossing for pedestrians would do. Carry on along the road to the main access and turn left. At the main road, go left again and begin to ascend the bridge which carries the road over the canal, the tramway and the railway. On the brow of the bridge there is a sign on the left directing you to the towpath. Descend thankfully to the canal bank, noting with some annoyance the tram stop you saw a little earlier, which is

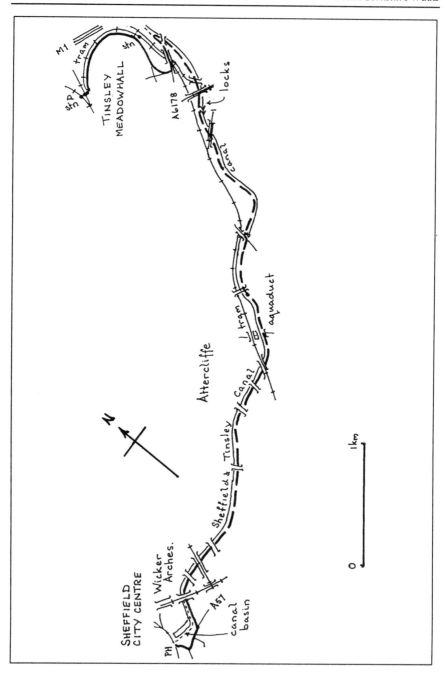

now only 100 metres away but separated from you by a couple of fences and a railway line.

Tinsley, despite its modern associations with steel works, shopping centres and motorways, is actually a very old settlement. The name is first recorded in Domesday. Where else? In 1086 it appears as "Tineslauue". The derivation is supposed to be "the mound or hill of a man called Tynni". However, the personal name element is again one of those only found in place names.

On the canal: kingfishers and oxygen

At the canal bank, turn right and at once pass under the main road bridge. Emerging from the bridge you will at once notice The Plumpers, an inn selling Stones ales. Fortunately for the safe continuation of this walk, the pub is on the opposite bank of the canal so you can't get to it unless you swim.

The towpath passes under Tinsley Road bridge, rebuilt in 1948 and now the first of the locks are encountered. It is immediately obvious that this is no narrow Midlands canal, but one of that group of wide canals associated with the Humber trade and the river navigations of the Don, the Aire and the Calder. It was at the first of these locks that the author encountered a kingfisher, which was a pleasant surprise, but indicative of how great an environmental change has taken place over the last few years.

An oxygen pipe spans the canal, not to provide assistance to walkers with respiratory difficulties, but to serve Edgar Allen's steel works on the far side of the canal. Industry and leisure now go hand in hand here, for in the pounds between the locks, there are marked bays for fishermen.

A deep lock is reached, followed by another bridge and more marked areas for fishermen. Two more locks and the towpath comes alongside the new tramway on the right. here the tramway shares the same alignment as the "ordinary" railway, though not the same rails. This was built by the South Yorkshire Railway and opened in 1864 shortly after the company had been taken over by its bigger neighbour the Manchester, Sheffield and Lincolnshire. It eventually closed to passenger traffic in 1970.

A changing economic base

The towpath passes a notice proclaiming the existence of the Sheffield Development Corporation, one of a number of initiatives started by the Government to regenerate areas like the Lower Don Valley. Thirty years ago this area was a land a steel works, foundries and factories. Now these industries have largely gone, leaving vast areas of dereliction and thousands of jobless people, but offering a chance to develop alternative uses that are not so environmentally damaging. Already there is a swathe of green along the canal bank and the water quality is good enough for fish. The new Lower Don developments may be more in keeping with the place names Attercliffe Common and Brightside, than their predecessors.

Level going

A further lock is followed by another bridge and another lock. Then comes an arched bridge and a length of boat moorings. Another lock lifts the canal above the surrounding land just sufficiently to enable a view right across the city to the blue line of the Peak District hills. Another line of moorings follows, then the final lock of the Tinsley flight. From here it is level all the way to the canal basin in the centre of Sheffield.

The new Sheffield Arena is in view at this point, just to the right, separated from the canal by the trams. Notice the remains of a lifting bridge on the left and see how many varieties of duck you can distinguish on the canal; rubber or plastic types excluded. A sign proclaims that you are in danger from overhead power lines, but this seems a little unlikely for the average-sized walker.

Soon Broughton Lane Bridge is reached. The plaque proclaims that this bridge was rebuilt in 1926. As elsewhere on the canal system this bridge has a number. This system was adopted on the succeeding railways and is still in use today. The numbering in this case starts from the canal basin in Sheffield. The original bridges simply have numbers, in this case 12. Later additions have a letter suffix. The towpath crosses the canal at this point, descending by a ramp or steps then curling left under the bridge. A turnover bridge of this type avoided the need to detach the tow rope from the horse. Another bridge soon crosses, this one carrying Coleridge Road over the canal. There is a seat here and a ramp up to the road. At a number of these access points there are discrete plaques informing you of the nearby presence of bus stops and hostelries. If you sampled all of the ones on offer, I have grave doubts that you would make the canal basin.

"Eric of Lincoln"

The next bridge is a new one, number 10a. This is the Brown Bayley Bridge, constructed in 1993 to serve the arena. It was at this point that the author saw the only moving boat during the whole walk. "Eric of Lincoln" came through the bridge laden down with dredgings, but conjuring up visions of a true working canal rather than a leisure waterway.

Soon there are more boat moorings and another bridge over the canal. Even here, so close to the heart of a city, there are trees of many varieties lining the waterway and making the walk a pleasant, almost rural experience. At Shirland Lane bridge there is a seat and an invitation to visit the Fox House Inn, which sells Stones beers. A wide area of canal now follows, where boats used to turn, moor and load. This was very muddy at the time the walk was reconnoitred. Presumably this was the origin of "Eric's" load.

An attractive cutting

Three bridges span an attractive cutting. lined with trees and shrubs. Some of the bridges themselves are very fine structures. Ignore all blandishments, like ramps which take you up the cutting side and continue along the towpath. The trams now cross over the canal on a new bridge, for at this point they have deserted the old railway formation and are running on a new route of their own. Seen from the tram, the approach to this bridge is very sharp. Indeed the new section of the tram alignment from here to the city centre has bends and gradients which are quite novel for passengers used to the gentle curves and grades of a railway.

Down in the canal cutting you see none of this, though you'll experience it on the way back.

A concrete bridge of 1926 vintage but numbered 7, carries Pinfold Lane over the canal. Staniforth Road Bridge soon follows, its plaque proclaiming the nearby presence of buses, food and ale. A ramp leads up to the road. Here, by the canal there is a seat and a landing stage, which serves the waterbus, when it is in operation. Hardy walkers like readers of this book should have no need of such assistance. The towpath now runs alongside a factory.

The remainder of the walk is wholly urban in feel, but interesting and enjoyable for all that. Notice the mooring bollards which have the date 1987 on them and the initials of the canal company, SSYN, the Sheffield and South Yorkshire Navigation. Keep your eyes open for a well-hidden milepost on the left which bears the distance 3 miles. From where, we wonders?

The next bridge passes under Bacon Lane. This is a delightful original arched bridge of 1819 vintage. As usual, there is a sign indicating that ale is available if you care to leave the canal to find it. Now look out for the remains of a canal branch on the right near Marriot's factory. There are remarkably few remains of this type on this canal, unlike the Birmingham system where there seem to be branches to every alternate house.

Into the City of Sheffield

The bridge carrying Bernard Road is a 1953 structure in concrete, boasting the number 5, so it is obviously a rebuild of an original. You are now drawing close to Sheffield city centre. Most people would predict that the derivation of the name Sheffield was "field by the river Sheaf". For once they would be justified. The name was first recorded in 1086 as "Scafeld", but the river name apparently comes from the Old English word "sceath", which meant "boundary". Until quite late in the 19th century the Derbyshire/Yorkshire boundary south of Heeley was the Sheaf. Nevertheless, it is rather curious the town took its name from the insignificant River Sheaf, rather than from the much more important Don.

Bridge number 4 carries the canal over the Midland Railway. This bridge has a date of 1870 on it, marking the date when the original Sheffield terminus of the Midland railway at Wicker was extended southwards to Chesterfield, via the new, more central station at Pond Street. The Royal Victoria Station Hotel can be seen to the right, almost on top of the railway viaduct which sweeps across the valley at this point. Cadman Street bridge is soon reached, another 1819 original. Now there are boats galore and another landing stage. At this point the railway viaduct, the famous Wicker Arches, crosses the canal. The viaduct carried the Manchester Sheffield and Lincolnshire Railway, across the Don valley to their main station at Victoria. This impecunious company was better known to its detractors as the Money Sunk and Lost Railway,

Temporary deviations

At this point there is a hiatus. As part of the major redevelopment of the canal basin, the towpath has been temporarily closed and a wall has been built across the alignment. As this is underneath the railway bridge there seems to be no way out, but on the left, in the bridge structure itself, there is an arch, dated 1846. This leads out into one of Sheffield's less salubrious back streets. Turn right here and go along the road in the direction of the new tram bridge, which can be seen ahead. As the road rises, there is a view through a gateway into the canal basin, with its magnificent warehouses straddling the water. At the main road turn right and followed the footway by the canal basin wall. Pass the frontage of the canal basin until you reach the pelican crossing at the end of Exchange Street. The Alexandra Hotel looks most inviting on the opposite side of the road. Cross with care! NB The towpath link into the rebuilt canal basin was due to be completed by Spring Bank Holiday 1995. Thereafter it should be possible to follow the canal through to its terminus and emerge onto the roadside almost opposite the Alexandra.

(To return to Tinsley, if you have left your car there, walk up Exchange Street, then left along Castle Street to the tram stop in Fitzallen Square. If you have a complex about being seen in a city in walking gear, take comfort from the author's example. Having walked in from Tinsley, my wife and I did a quick change act in the pub and then went shopping in the city, carrying our walking tackle, including the rucksack, in a Lewis's carrier bag!)

27. Ulley Country Park

The Route: Ulley Country Park, Ulley Reservoir, Reservoir Road, Ulley village, Carr Lane, High Lane, Ulley Hall Farm, Ulley village (again), Ulley Lane, Ulley Country Park.

Distance: 8.5km (5.3 miles)

Start: Visitor Centre at Ulley Reservoir. GR 876452

Map(s): OS 1:25000 Pathfinder Series No. 744, Aughton and Carlton in Lindrick

How to get there:

By public transport: Bus services from Sheffield, Rotherham and Chesterfield pass the entrance to the visitor centre

By car: Follow the main A618 from Rotherham or from its junction with the A57 at Swallownest. Ulley Country Park is signed from the main road, but the junction is awkward because of fast moving traffic.

The Walk

Ulley Country Park

Either at the start or end of this walk, make a point of visiting the information centre. It has an excellent display about the reservoir and how it came to be a country park. Just before the information centre, go left and drop down the path almost to the lakeside. Here turn left again and follow the path round until it reaches the dam. A flight of steps takes you onto the crest of the dam, from which vantage point you'll get a panoramic view of the lake, with its attendant fishermen. When the walk was reconnoitred the fishermen had been joined by a family of Great Crested Grebes. Both seemed to coexist quite happily, though who was catching the most was impossible to say. There was a surprising amount of wildlife on and around this little lake despite its obvious popularity with visitors. At least two different types of dragonfly were spotted and half a dozen different wildfowl. Added to that, the fishermen shared this tiny patch of water with a flotilla of sailing dinghies, who no sooner turned round one buoy than they were approaching another.

Go along the crest of the dam and then cross the overflow channel on the bridge thoughtfully provided. The path now follows the edge of the lake, with a fence on the left separating you from the road. Where the road crosses the reservoir, the path passes through a kissing gate. Cross the road and go through another kissing gate along a less populated arm of the reservoir. There is a fence on the left and a ditch, so the path maintains a constrained course with water either side.

Continue along the path, which soon swings right to cross the inlet stream on a bridge. There is some evidence of people straying from the path at this point and

Ulley reservoir

heading upstream, but ignore this and continue on the marked path. The path rounds
the head of the lake and begins its traverse of the southern edge. This section passes
through a patch of gorse and when the author and his wife researched the route, their
passage was marked by a continuous crackling, like distant rifle fire. This turned out
to be the seed pods of the gorse, bursting in the heat. In places, paths head off into
the gorse, sheer masochism in my view. The lower, waymarked route by the lake is
much easier. The blackberries are better too.

An extensive view

A wall separates the path from the water and eventually a dead tree is reached. Here
you are away from the gorse and on a more open hillside. Bear left here, going steeply
up the hill, leaving the lakeside path behind. Minor paths head off left and right but
you should ignore these and carry on upwards to reach a clump of hawthorns. This
marks the edge of the country park and there is quite an extensive view back over
Orgreave and the Rother valley. Beyond this point you are in fields. Keeping the
hedge to your left, carry straight on towards the white house.

The hedge on the left is broken in places to reveal a rough lane. The official access
to this is through a gateway near the end of the field. Carry on along the lane, passing
the white house you saw earlier, which rejoices in the unimaginative name of White
Cottage. Soon the lane reaches the road and here you go left. This is Reservoir Road.
A sign by the side of the road proclaims that the lane along which you have come is
the access to Harris Quarries, specialists in fireplaces. Just the place to come on a

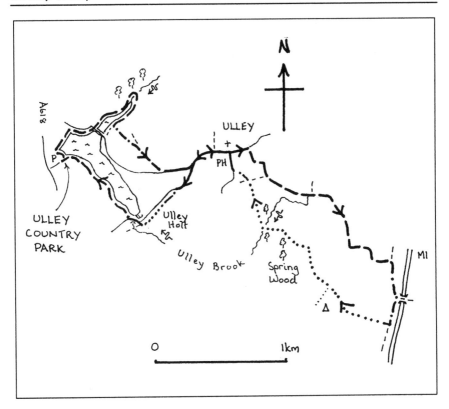

cold winter's day. Ahead, over the fields, can be seen the spire of Aston church, but your route lies to the left, along the road to Ulley.

Ulley village – first visit

At the road junction near the bus shelter go left along Main Street and enter Ulley village. Like so many place names, this first appears in Domesday in 1086, where it is rendered as "Ollei". It is reputed to mean "the woodland clearing frequented by owls", but given the proximity of the various motorways nowadays, you will be lucky to see or hear an owl. Nevertheless it is a lovely village. As you pass West End Farm, note the old pump on the left. Ignore the various footpath signs on the left and carry straight on, passing Holy Trinity church on the left and the old school on the right. Just before the junction of Main Street and Turnshaw Road there is a good view of the back of the Royal Oak pub. Most commercial buildings seen from the rear present a rather poor aspect, but this is an exception. It backs straight onto fields, there is no accumulated junk, just a pony nuzzling up to one of the lower windows. A great pity there's no access to the pub this way, but no matter, carry on to Turnshaw Road and there turn right. The pub is just on the right.

Benny Hill Lane?

Possibly having duly imbibed, retrace your steps to the Main Street and turn right by the West Riding signpost. After a couple of hundred metres Carr Lane goes off to the right, just by the pumping station. Notice that the road you are on seems to be called Benny Hill Lane according to the nameplate. I suspect the map is more correct here in calling the route Penny Hill Lane!

Turn right, down Carr Lane, your view now taking in the junction of the M1 and M18 motorways. Despite the proximity of these major roads, the walk along Carr Lane is very pleasant and the route has a timeless feel about it. Carr Lane describes an S bend and then after about another 100 metres a track joins from the right. This does not appear on the Pathfinder map and should be ignored. Carr Lane continues, a lovely green road, hedge lined, but with plenty of evidence of the dreaded Dutch Elm disease. You pass a new shed on the left, which on closer inspection turns out to be a stable. Then the lane goes sharply to the right. From here on the lane is very narrow, with overgrown hedges either side, but with a fine population of butterflies. However, you are now getting very close to the motorway and the incessant buzz of traffic begins to intrude. Again there are dead elms on this stretch, but also plenty of other hedgerow trees, particularly oak and ash.

The lane turns sharply to the left and now the motorway junction is so close you can almost read the signs. A further twist to the right and then to the left brings you to a stretch with crab apple trees and some rather incongruous concrete inspection covers. Some insensitive soul has decided to burn down parts of the hedges. This devastation continues until you reach a T-junction where Carr Lane joins High Lane. Both are green lanes. Here you go right and pass over a stile.

The elusive "north"

Keep alongside the hedge, which has again been partially burnt out. The path is now getting perilously close to the motorway, which is now less than 100 metres away to the left, but hidden by a tree screen. The field narrows and in the corner there is another stile. The path now enters motorway territory and climbs the embankment. Fear not. You are not being asked to run across 8 lanes of fast moving traffic, for at the top of the embankment there is a bridge to the left over the M1. However, this is not your route. The track you want continues straight ahead, by the M1, descending the embankment to the fields again.

On your left there is a wonderful example of duplicate signing. A huge advance direction sign warns of the impending M1/M18 junction. A few metres further, there is a near identical sign, the only obvious addition being the elusive place "The North". Travels around the country suggest that this first appears on signs in Dover and continues to appear until somewhere near Thurso, when it finally disappears.

At the stile near the base of the embankment there is a footpath sign and here you go right, heading straight across the field, away from the motorway, making to the left of the lattice tower. A post in the hedge ahead marks the position of the stile. Once through the stile, a quick left and right brings you alongside a hedge. Carry on, still making towards the lattice tower. The tower of Aston Church, an altogether more solid and inspiring structure, can be seen away to the left. The view ahead is a surprise, for you are high enough at this point to see over the towns of the Rother and Don valleys to the higher hills of the Peak District and the back of Sheffield.

Act of faith, or pious hope?

Just before the pylon there is a footpath sign in the hedge on the left. This points diagonally across the field lying to your right. It takes rather an act of faith to launch out across the field, for the other side cannot be seen at this point. If you stand with your back to the signpost and head off across the field diagonally left, in ten paces you will breast the rise and see the footpath sign at the opposite side. You will also pick out more distant landmarks like Emley Moor television mast and Laughton en le Morthen church spire.

At the footpath sign bear left, following the remains of a field boundary on your right. When the author walked this path it was something of a struggle, for the farmer had ploughed right to the extremity of the field and left nowhere to walk other than in the furrows.

Soon another footpath sign is reached, pointing across the field to your right. Head diagonally left across the field, making for the white house and the oak tree. At the oak tree go left, with a hedge on your right. When the path reaches the belt of trees, it passes through a gap in the hedge and runs down through the scrub, before emerging in open fields again. This section does not show clearly on the Pathfinder map and nor does the next bit, for the path drops straight down the field to a thin belt of trees that border the stream. The trees are not shown on the map and there does not appear to be an obvious way through. However, just to the left of the fourth oak there is a well-hidden gap which leads to a stone clapper bridge.

Go over the bridge and up the steps on the opposite side, to come back into open fields again. Bear diagonally right here, up the slope to the left of the tree belt. Soon the path crests the rise to reveal Ulley and the farm buildings ahead and to the left. The path heads towards the yellow bungalow and the right-hand end of the farm buildings. Cross the prominent track, which was not on your map earlier on and therefore is unlikely to be so now. Here the path bears left, to skirt the farm and reach a stile in the wall at the right-hand end of the barn.

Ulley village – second visit

Go over the stile and turn right, reaching the road near the gate to Ulley Hall Farm. The pub is now reached for the second time. Pick up any stragglers who refused to sample the delights of Carr Lane and preferred those of Sam Smiths and again make your way to Main Street. This time turn left. At the junction of Ulley Lane, Reservoir Road and Main Street, go straight ahead, down Ulley Lane. This rapidly develops into a substantial holloway, with neither verge nor footway. Fortunately for all concerned, there is a waymarked stile on the left which leads into the adjacent field. Once in the field, the path closely follows the right-hand hedge, with the holloway deep below. The path descends easily to reach a stile in the corner of the field. Carry on over another stile, passing the picnic tables and so reach the road again.

The back door to Ulley Country Park

Cross the road with care and go through the kissing gate into the southern end of Ulley Country Park. Go left, passing over the bridge which spans Ulley Brook. Ignore the path which joins from the left, but continue along the lakeside, a very pleasant stroll back to the visitor centre. Tram fanatics should look out for the tram rail embedded in a concrete bridge en route to the visitor centre.

28. Woodsetts

The Route: Lindrick Hill, Anston Stones Wood, Little Stones, Rackford Lane, Dewidales Wood, Woodsetts, Socheage Hill, Lindrick Golf Course, Lindrick Bridge.

Distance: 7km (4.35 miles)

Start: Either from Lindrick Hill, where there is a bus stop and a large layby, just by the entrance to Anston Stones Wood GR 537828, or, for public transport users, from Woodsetts, where the bus stop is adjacent to the Butchers Arms.

Map(s): OS 1:25000 Pathfinder Series No. 744, Aughton and Carlton in Lindrick

How to get there:

By public transport: Daily bus services from Rotherham to Worksop serve the stop on Lindrick Hill. A Monday to Saturday service between Dinnington and Worksop serves the village of Woodsetts.

By car: the layby is on the north side of the main A57 trunk road, a little over a mile east of South Anston cross roads. Cars approaching from the Worksop direction will have to cross the flow of traffic to reach the layby. Traffic moves very fast on this stretch of road. The layby is near the brow of a hill so visibility is not good. If you can approach from South Anston direction, do so.

The Walk

Quick exit from the A57

From the lay by on the A57 walk down the hill until you reach the entrance to Anston Stones Wood. Public transport users will have to walk across Lindrick "Bridge" and up to the entrance, slightly further than the car user, but at least when you re-emerge onto the A57 later on you haven't got a final bit of uphill to contend with.

Anston Stones Wood

There is an information board at the entrance to the wood. The board states that Anston parish council own the wood and that it is cared for by a consortium. You will agree as you go through the valley that they are doing an excellent job. The information board also makes the astonishing claim that 1375 different species of plants and animals have been found in the wood over the last twenty years.

Go through the gate into the wood, leaving the roar of the A57 behind. This is a truly delightful deciduous woodland, growing on limestone. The path is broad and easily followed. Just past a clearing, by a large beech, the track begins to dip into the dale bottom and soon comes alongside the Anston Brook. Continue along the broad

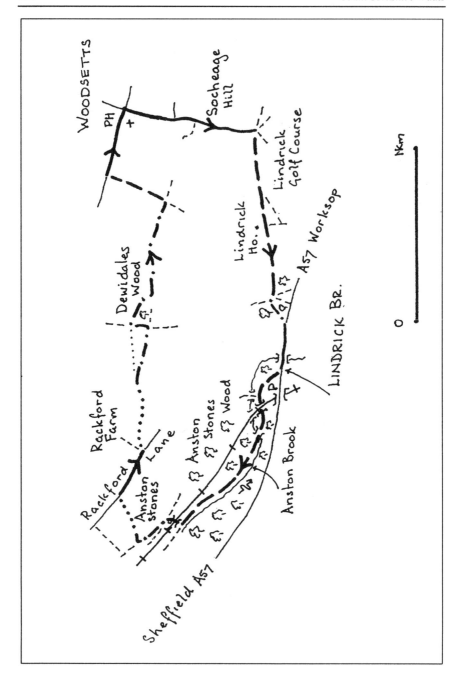

path until you reach a junction. You can go either way at this point, as the information board makes clear, but the route of this walk is to the left, under the railway bridge. You will be lucky to see a train, for this line was mainly built to serve the collieries in the area. Coal mines being an endangered species, there are now few trains. In this the information board is wrong, for it describes the line as built by the early railway pioneers as a passenger route. It was in fact quite a late line, only opening in October 1905 and although it did carry a passenger service from 1910, this ceased as early as 1929. As you pass under the bridge, note the fine skew brick arch.

Continue along the path. The wood is superb and has the feel of one of the better Derbyshire Dales, except that it isn't so busy. Soon the path forks again. As before you can take either route, but the described walk bears right. Cross the brook by the bridge and, ignoring numerous little paths going off left and right, ascend gently. The railway is just to your right, well-hidden in the trees. The noise of the A57 still manages to permeate down into the valley bottom, but it is muffled and not obtrusive.

Ignore the obvious path to the right, under the railway bridge and carry straight on. The path now descends slightly, almost to river level again. Here there is a bridge over the stream and those who ignored the advice of the author at the last major junction now rejoin the walk route. Those who have remained faithful to the route described should ignore the bridge and carry straight on.

A use for old sleepers

A short way beyond the river bridge the path forks again. Turn right here, to pass under the railway bridge. A clear path then ascends, quite steeply, away from the railway. It must have been a scramble to use this path at one time, but not now. The consortium who manage the wood have installed steps made out of old railway sleepers. Unlike many steps installed in countryside locations, these are at the correct spacing and height for easy use. There's even a hand rail! At the top of the steps you come out onto a "landing" made out of a limestone wall. Here you join another path which comes in from the right. Go left here, but ignore the next left fork in the path. Instead go up the flight of steps a little way further on and again on the left.

Little Stones and indistinct paths

At the top of the steps a narrow but well-trodden path keeps to the edge of the wood – ignore any paths leading left. The path soon drops through a gap in the boundary wall into open fields. Here you go left, through waist high grass interspersed with bushes. This is the area shown on the map as Little Stones. It is a rough hummocky area with small outcrops of limestone breaking through the vegetation. Nevertheless, the path is distinct, though it soon forks. Here you go right, heading to the right of the solitary oak "bush", making a bee-line for the dead tree seen ahead. The path runs through a shallow "cutting" of limestone. As you emerge you can see the spire of South Anston church away to the left. Keep your eyes peeled for a crossing of paths and when you find it, turn right. The crossing is not distinct, but lies about midway between the oak and the dead tree. The straight on route is far more obvious.

Having made the right turn, follow the path as it twists its way towards another dead tree. Most of these dead trees seem to be elms, which have suffered from the ravages of Dutch Elm disease. As the path nears the dead tree, you seem to be faced with an impenetrable thicket of blackthorn. However, there is a clear path straight through the middle to a stile in the fence. Beyond is farmland and a clear path crosses the field to another stile on the far side, just to the left of the electricity pylon with the extra bit on top. This second stile deposits you onto Rackford Lane.

An alternative

(If you miss the crossing of paths mentioned in the last two paragraphs, don't despair, but carry straight on towards the first dead tree. The path soon passes into the shade of a thicket of thorn, in the midst of which there is a junction of paths and a gatepost. Go through the kissing gate on the right. Follow the fence and hedge on your left to another kissing gate which takes you out onto Rackford Lane).

Rackford Lane

Turn right, along the lane, which is lined with elm bushes, many of which are in the grip of the dreaded Dutch Elm disease. A notice on the right proclaims that the field through which you have just passed is available for public access and has been sown with wild flower seeds to try and recreate a limestone grassland. Should be a sight for sore eyes. The lane is tarmac for about 300 metres, but the surfacing ceases at the entrance to Rackford Farm. There is an extensive view ahead towards Worksop.

Good balance needed

Just beyond the farm drive and the new house, there is a stile on the left, which is signposted. Go over the stile and keep by the fence on the left to another stile by a water trough. Be very careful here. The water trough is full of water and the stile is amongst the most rickety the author has ever encountered.

Having surmounted this obstacle you enter a field in which there are horses grazing. The author has a healthy respect for horses. For one thing, they can certainly outrun you and they have a tendency to be over-frisky. When this walk was reconnoitred the horses were so hot that they couldn't be bothered to raise their heads, let alone run, but you have been warned. The path, fortunately does not go over towards the stables, but bears right.

Head diagonally across the field to the stile which can be seen in the far right-hand corner. This is a curious field. A shallow valley runs away to the right, lined on the northern side by thorns. The path avoids the valley and keeps to the left of the thorns. There is no obvious path on the ground, even when you near the stile.

Deviations on a theme of paths

Once over this stile you can see a woodland ahead. This is Dewidales Wood. The map shows the right of way heading across the field to reach the left-hand corner of the wood. This is not what happens in practice. A well-beaten path heads straight for the right-hand end of the wood, obviously following an old field boundary. On reaching the wood there was no sign of a path to the left, but a well-blazed route led straight on, with the wood to the left. In a few metres, you reach a broad track, which is the bridleway from Lindrick Common to the Dinnington Road. Turn left here, into the wood, noting that the path you have just used seems to carry on alongside the wood, despite what the map says.

Go through the wood and emerge on the northern side. Here there should be evidence of a path on the left, the one you should have followed. There isn't, but there is a footpath signpost which points back through the wood the way you have just come. There is also a signpost pointing right. Follow this path alongside the top of the wood. Woodsetts is now in view ahead. Suspicion is aroused when the path, still following the boundary of the wood, bends to the right. To your annoyance you will find a path trailing in from the right where the wood ends. This is not shown on the map, nor is it a right of way, but it is a continuation of the path you were on about five minutes earlier when you first entered the wood and it cuts off two sides of a triangle. Still you can console yourself with the fact that you have virtuously followed the correct line.

The path bends left at the end of the wood and continues along the field boundary to another small stand of trees, which are un-named on the map. The 1:25000 map shows a left and right-hand kink in the path at the far end of the wood. At the end of the wood turn left and walk into the field for about 40 paces, with your eyes on the right-hand end of the wood seen in the distance. After 40 paces turn right, heading for a solitary bush at the far end of the field. This was surprisingly clear on the ground, despite there being crops growing and no field boundary to follow.

Via Holly Bush to Woodsetts

At the solitary bush, which turns out to be a holly, you reach a track. If you are going to the Butchers Arms pub, go left here. (If you are not going to the pub you can carry straight on and avoid the village). Follow the track until it bears away to the left. An older version of the track continues ahead as a green and grassy path, with the fence and hedge on the right. Note the sign proclaiming that the horses in the adjacent field are freeze marked. This apparently has nothing to do with the temperature in these parts, but is an attempt to prevent the horses being stolen. Probably by the time you visit the area, the sign itself will have been nicked.

At the end of the path you reach the Anston to Woodsetts road and turn right into the village.

Woodsetts

The name Woodsetts first appears as late as 1324 where it is referred to as "Wodesete". The derivation is nevertheless from the Old English "wudu" and "set", meaning the "(sheep)fold in the wood". Not that there is much sign of sheep now, nor of any sheepfold. The Butchers Arms lies in the centre of the village, at the crossroads.

From the pub, cross the main road and go down Lindrick Road, with St George's church on your right. As churches go, this one is relatively modern, being built in 1841. However, there was almost certainly a church of some description earlier than this. Note the unusual memorial clock on the south face of the church. Continue down Lindrick Road, passing a new stable block. (The footpath sign here marks the

Woodsetts church and the Butchers Arms

point at which non pub-users will rejoin the walk, having come across the field from the holly tree). The road now narrows appreciably and there is no footway. Fortunately there is not much traffic either. The lane climbs quite sharply up the slopes of Socheage Hill, which betrays its limestone heritage in the shallow cutting at the top. An equally sharp drop down the south side takes you to the edge of Lindrick Golf Course.

Nirvana for some; A57 for others

Pass through the gateway and turn right, following the bridleway sign. Nirvana is soon reached, but turns out to be unobtainable by ordinary walkers. Pass it by. The broad track continues past other large houses with good views over the golf course. After Wildways, the track forks. Keep to the right-hand track, passing along the front of a few more houses. Ignore the bridleway sign signpost on the left, which will only lead you onto the main road too soon and continue ahead. After Maltkiln House, the track narrows to a green lane, hedged on either side.

Soon you reach the edge of a wood. The OS map shows a path bearing away left here, and indeed there is evidence of it, but it doesn't go far. Instead, take the more obvious path to the right. This soon reaches a further track, by a gateway into a field on your right. Ignoring the gateway and the track, plunge ahead into the wood on a sketchy path. This winds its way through the trees until it reaches a gap in the boundary wall. Here you drop neatly onto the verge of the A57, quite close to the Lindrick Hill bus stop. A quick sprint along the road to the right takes you over Lindrick Bridge, though you'll not notice it, and back to your car.

29. Worrall

The Route: Worrall, Low Ash Farm, Low Ash Common, Haighen Field, Spitewinter Farm, Burnt Hill Lane, Coumes Farm, Coumes Vale Plantation, Onesacre, Coldwell, The Asplands, Worrall.

Distance: 7.75km (4.8 miles)

Start: Worrall car park. GR 305922

Map(s): OS 1:25000 Pathfinder Series No. 726 Sheffield (N) and Stocksbridge

How to get there:

By public transport: There is a daily and relatively frequent service to Worrall from Sheffield, with a stop by the Blue Ball.

By car: From the north follow the A616 to the one way system round Oughtibridge. Go almost the whole way round the one way system to the sign for Worrall on the left. Continue to follow the Worrall signs, taking care not to miss the left turn about 3/4 km from the A616. The follow this road as it climbs steadily up to Worrall. At the Blue Bell turn sharp right up Towngate Lane, bearing right at the next junction with Top Road. The car park is about 150 metres further on the left. From the south follow the A616 from Sheffield to Middlewood. Worrall is signed to the left just past the hospital complex. At the T-junction in Worrall turn left and join the route from the north about 200 metres before the Blue Ball pub.

The Walk

Worrall

The place name Worrall is thought to derive from the Old English "wir" and "halh", which together mean "the nook of land where bog myrtle grows". Not that you'll find any on the car park, but if you spot any on the walk, please let me know. From the car park retrace your steps down to the Blue Ball. (If you are not calling in, proceed along Top Road, past the Shoulder of Mutton to reach Long Lane). From the Blue Ball go right and then right again up Kirk Edge Road, passing the troughs on the right.

Climb Kirk Edge Road until it joins Top Road and changes name to Long Lane. Continue up Long Lane, passing Worrall Hall Farm on the right, a fine old building. Just past the cross roads of Long Lane with Kirk Edge Drive and Briarfields Lane, by a school sign, there is a footpath sign on the left.

The footpath is very narrow, hemmed in on the left by a house and on the right by a field wall. The path appears to go nowhere, seemingly end in a blank wall. However, just as you think you have been led astray even more than usual, you come to a flight of steps on the right. These take you into the field. Head diagonally to the left across the field keeping the rough ground to the left. You should find a stile in the far wall by the pylon, though the path is far from clear. In the next field continue bearing left to reach a stile in the far left-hand corner. Do not go through the gate.

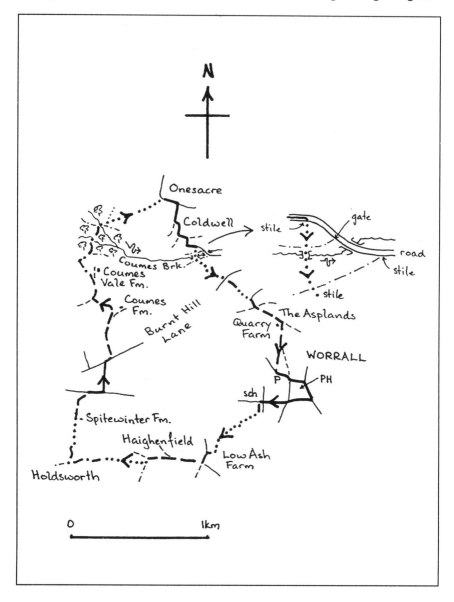

A grand view

Keep to the left of the water works enclosure in this next field to reach a stile in the middle of the top wall. Once through this stile the path turns right and follows the wall until another stile is reached. There is a good view to the right from here, for you have climbed quite a way above Worrall. The view takes in the Don Valley and the lower end of Wharncliffe Woods and Crags. Beyond the stile the path bears left, heading diagonally across the field to a further stile in the far left-hand corner, between two gateways. Once through the stile carry on with the wall on your left, heading towards Low Ash Farm. The path reaches the farm by a stile adjacent to a gate. This lands you on a rough track, where you go right. This farm was at one time a boarding school for the "sons of gentlemen".

Follow the track until you reach the lane and then go left. Follow the road for about 100 metres, until it swings sharp left. Two tracks diverge here. Yours is the one to the right, not straight on, which is the more obvious of the two at first. The track goes through a gateway and runs alongside grassed over old workings to the right. This is Low Ash Common. Ahead and to the left there are extensive views, for you are looking up the valleys that contain Agden and Damflask reservoirs towards Bradfield and Derwent Edge.

The track forks, but keep to the left-hand way, alongside the wall. After another 150 metres, look out for a footpath sign on the left, just beyond the clump of bushes. The obvious track continuing ahead is not a right of way, so go left, over the stile into the small field. Another stile quickly follows and the path forks at a signpost. Turn right, alongside the wall, where there are remnants of a paved path. The path continues through a series of fields, always with the wall to the right, the stile in the corner and evidence of old paving. The path passes below Haighen Field Farm on the right and the site of an old air shaft on the left.

An easily-missed junction

At another stile the path leaves the fields and enters an area of bracken and scrub before going left, then right, alongside the barbed wire fence. The scrub becomes a well-established woodland, through which the path passes, way marked in places. The bracken and rosebay willowherb was shoulder high when the walk was reconnoitred and the path twisted and turned through the jungle, but was always obvious. Keep a sharp look out for a waymarker on the right, just opposite a rowan tree. (The waymarker is easily missed, but if you do miss it you will soon reach a stile at the end of the wood. If you reach the stile you have come too far, so turn round and retrace your steps for about 20 metres). At the waymarker go right, (left if you're retracing your steps). There is no obvious path through the shoulder high bracken, but head for a point just to the left of the birch tree, where a narrow path becomes clear. This climbs up to the top of a little scarp to reach a waymarker post. This indicates a path straight on, which is your route. It also indicates a route to the right, which is odd as there is nothing shown on the map in this direction. Still musing on this, go straight on to reach a stile which takes you into open fields again.

Carry straight on across the field to the wall corner, then follow the wall, keeping it to your left. Pass through a stile and continue to follow the wall on the left to reach a gate just to the left of Spitewinter Farm. The track from the farm now crests the rise and opens up a view towards Wharncliffe Woods and the Don Valley. Follow the track across the fields, bearing right to reach a gate onto Long Lane. Turn right here and go down the road for about 150 metres until you reach a junction. This is signed Oughtibridge and Wharncliffe Side. Go left here, descending along this minor road, with good views ahead over Coumes Vale and the Upper Don Valley. At the T-junction at the bottom of the lane go right.

Coumes Vale

After a very short distance you pass under a power line and there is a seat, stile and footpath sign on the left. The footpath is not marked as a right of way on the author's map, but it is signposted as such here and it features in one of Sheffield City Council's walks leaflets, so it must be accurate. Go over the stile and descend the track towards Coumes Farm, beyond which is the lovely wooded valley of Coumes Vale. The approach to the farm is marred by a collection of farm junk and derelict vehicles. The reuse of pallets as a gate shows innovation, but is not the easiest barrier to surmount.

As the track nears the farm, there is a fork and you keep left. The track now rises away from the farm, still swinging left, to reach a gateway into a field. Still ascending gently the track runs through the field, with the remains of a fence on the left and a wood to the right. There were frisky bullocks in the field when the reconnoitre took place. As it was clear that the remnant fence was neither use nor ornament, the author found himself calculating how far away the woodland edge was and whether he could reach it before being caught by the cattle. Mercifully this strenuous exercise was not put to the test. The track bears right at the end of the field, to reach a stile by a gate. Do not let your relief at escaping the cattle get the better of you, for the stile is precariously close to a very deep ditch.

Go right at the rough lane and descend towards Coumes Vale Farm. Continuing to muse on farmers' propensity to put machinery out to grass, you will find yourself in the farm yard. If so, you have gone too far, for the right of way bears left, just before the barn. Make your way along the back of the barn, avoiding the dumped farm machinery. The hillside rises steeply on the left, so there's no escape that way. The wall slopes up to the left but carry straight on to reach a stile by a gate. This is waymarked! Go right here, following the wall down the field, across the boggy patch by the gateway. Ignore the stile on the right and keep alongside the wall, which now bears left into woodland. A vegetation filled hollow way soon materialises on your left, but a clear path now develops, under the trees. Note the waymarker on one of the oaks. Pass through an open glade, with a fence to the right and continue through the wood to reach a waymarked stile. Beyond the stile the ground is wet and muddy, so much so that some considerate soul has installed stepping stones.

Still traversing the obvious path through the trees, you reach a stile by a gate. Ignore the path to the left, but continue ahead across more muddy ground and a stream. Just beyond the stream there is a ladder stile by a gate, followed almost at once by a further stile in the wall.

By deviant routes

Beyond this point the boundary walls and fences bear little relationship to those shown on the map and the walked line of the path seems to vary from the mapped route as well, though there is not much evidence of either. From the stile, the walked route heads across the field to reach the far wall, at which point it turns right and follows the wall to a ladder stile by a gateway. (The authorised line keeps to the left-hand edge of the field as far as the wall, then goes right, following the wall to the ladder stile). From the ladder stile carry straight on, across the field to another ladder stile in the corner, not through the gateway on the right. In the next field the intermediate boundaries have all been removed and the walked line of the path makes a bee line for yet another ladder stile, which can be seen in the trees above the buildings. Once over this ladder stile you reach Onesacre and a lane. Here you go right.

Onesacre

Onesacre is a fine collection of old buildings on both sides of the road. Particularly noticeable is the cruck barn on the right, which is still in use. The old school house apparently dates back to 1100, but presumably it was not a school house then. Follow the road down to the junction and there turn right. A rare sign survival from the "good old days" of motoring proclaims that the hill you are descending is 1 in 4.5 and that there are bends for 1/4 mile. Very true. The lane descends steeply in a deep cut holloway, with trees on either side. Note the eucalyptus tree on the left, in the garden of a house. At Coldwell Farm the road emerges from the holloway and bears right, still descending quite steeply.

Eyes right for a well-hidden stile

The lane now bends to the left with hedges either side. Less than 100 metres beyond the bend, look out for a stile on the right. It is well-disguised and unsigned, hidden by a large ash tree and the hedge. Go through the stile and then straight down the field to locate a bridge by the tallest ash tree.

If you miss the stile from the road, don't despair, but carry on down the lane to the bottom and go right, through the unsigned gateway just before the bridge carrying the road over the stream. A path alongside the stream takes you to the footbridge mentioned earlier. The author admits to missing both these alternatives on the reconnoitre and having to make do with a third version, which is a signed path on the right, just beyond the road bridge. Some backtracking was then necessary to establish the credentials of the true route.

Up to Coldwell

Once over the footbridge there is an obvious stile in the right-hand top corner of the field. Obvious, but wrong. Instead scramble up the bank onto the more level part of the field and thus find a stile in the wall ahead, just by a sycamore tree. Go through the stile and follow the wall on your right. The wall curves gently to the left to reach a gateway and stile. Go right, not straight on at this point and soon reach another stile, on the left, between two beech trees. Now follow the wall on your left and so reach a small gate and stile in the corner of the field. Ignore the more obvious, larger gateway. The path keeps on the left-hand side of the farm buildings, with a view across the valley to Wharncliffe Lodge and Brownlow Rocher. A gateway leads out onto the road where you should turn right and immediately left, up a footpath signed to Worrall. The footpath follows a narrow driveway alongside a building that was in the process of being restored when the reconnoitre took place. At the end of the drive there is a flight of steps and a little gate leading back into fields. Go straight on here, with the field wall to your right, ignoring the inviting gateway.

The path, which displays evidence of paving in places, continues alongside the wall on the right, passing through a couple of stiles. At the top of the field, to the right of the new barn, the path emerges onto a track. Go right here, following the walled, rough lane. In a short distance, by a trough on the right, there is a crossing of tracks and paths, with a goodly supply of signposts. Go straight on here, climbing quite steeply. Once past the big gateposts on the right the path levels out. On the left are the infilled remains of an old quarry, now well vegetated.

Asplands and Worrall

The path runs along the lip of the former quarry until the house called Asplands is reached. Just beyond the house there is a stile on the right, by a gate. This is your route. The path cuts straight across the field heading towards the houses of Worrall and the white gate. There should be no difficulty in route finding here, as the path is well-blazed. Just past the white gate and the troughs on the right, the path becomes a narrow walled lane. Continue along the lane until it forks. The left-hand fork goes towards the pubs and buses . That to the right leads up past the new houses to emerge on the road close to the car park.

30. Worsbrough Country Park

The Route: Worsbrough Country Park, Worsbrough Bridge, Canal Basin, Park Cottages, Worsbrough village, New Plantation, Rockley Dike, Worsbrough reservoir, Worsbrough Country Park.

Distance: 5km (3.1 miles)

Start: Worsbrough Country Park GR 351033

Map(s): OS 1:25000 Pathfinder Series No. 715 Barnsley and Penistone.

How to get there:

By public transport: A frequent daily service passes the main access to the country park, from Barnsley and Sheffield.
By car: Follow the A61 from Barnsley, Sheffield or the M1 at Tankersley. The access to the country park is signed, though it is an awkward entrance.

The Walk

Worsbrough Country Park

Either before the walk, or on your way back, you should visit the information centre and mill museum in the country park. There is a wealth of information available about the area, which a book of this nature cannot hope to emulate. Perhaps the best thing to do is to pay a quick visit before you start walking, and to pay a more leisurely visit on your way back.

From the entrance to the country park, opposite the Red Lion, go left along the A61 and cross the River Dove. Just over the bridge, cross the road, with care. Walk past the garage and then go right, through a gateway into the eastern part of the country park. Ahead is the canal basin, the terminus of the erstwhile Dearne and Dove Canal. In its hey day this was a busy industrial canal, carrying coal, iron and manufactured goods as well as foodstuffs. It is hard to envisage that now, for the clear still waters are devoid of boats, there are no warehouses or obvious signs of industry, just a green sward stretching down to the bank. On the bank there is likely to be plenty of life though, for this is a popular fishing spot. Walkers are much in evidence too, though not the booted, anorak-wearing, rucksack weighted variety.

Danger! Thin ice

Keep to the left of the canal and carry on along the towpath. Just past the electricity sub station, note the lifebuoy on the opposite bank. Note particularly the sign which accompanies it, which proclaims, "Danger thin ice". When this walk was reconnoitred there had just been a long dry and hot spell, so any ice must indeed have been thin!

A little further on the canal ends abruptly. The alignment can be seen carrying on

Worsborough Basin

down the valley, but your route diverges here. Go across the canal and then bear right, descending to reach a footbridge over the Dove.

Machete wielders to the fore

Cross the river and make your way under the trees, up the steps to the point where the path forks. At the fork keep left, up another few steps until the overgrown entrance to a hollow way is encountered. The path seems to fork here, one branch going up the hollow way, the other bearing right into the field. Although the map seems to indicate that the hollow way is the correct route, the author can vouch for the impassability of this way. After a few metres all trace of a path vanishes amidst nettles, scrub and other rampant vegetation. Go into the field instead and keeping the hollow way on your left, make your way up along the path. A hedge divides the field from the hollow way, but you can occasionally glimpse a veritable jungle down in the bottom. Clearly no path there.

Still keeping alongside the hedge, the path bears right and dips to reach a track which crosses the hollow way. The hollow way continues ahead, but is blocked by a fence. If your suspicions have not been aroused before, they should be now, for this is no medieval pack horse route, but the remains of a railway winding incline, for carrying coal down from the nearby colliery to the canal. Looking up the "hollow way", you can see the spoil heap of the colliery, now graded down and grass covered. Turn right along the crossing track.

As the track rises, you can see the colliery site more clearly. It has been reworked as an opencast site more recently, but has now been restored. Hoyland church is also

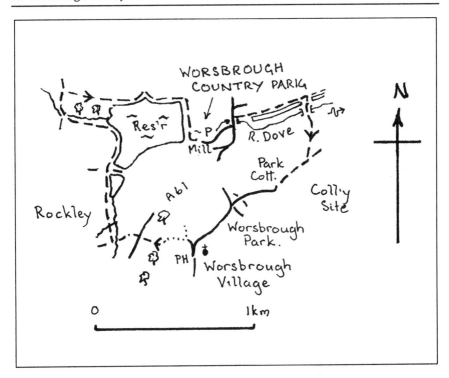

in view up to the left. Soon the track joins a rough lane, which has obviously seen use by the opencast vehicles, but is now virtually traffic free. Pass through the gate and follow the lane up, passing Park Cottages on your right. Soon you will see footpath signs to left and right, but ignore these and carry on along the lane. In about 100 metres you reach the road and here go left, up the hill towards Worsbrough village.

Into Worsbrough village – at a gallop!

Keep on the footway on the left-hand side of the road, passing the disused round-about, which again seems to have been associated with the colliery or open cast. As you approach the village, Worsbrough Park is to your left and Worsbrough Hall to the right. The footpath sign on the left seems to point into jungle, but fortunately your way lies up the road not along the footpath. At this point, there is a curious sign which seems to indicate that elderly people have got to slow down to 5 mph. This seems to be a curious request bearing in mind that even the fastest walker finds it hard to maintain 4 mph for any distance.

The road now narrows so much that it has to be controlled by traffic lights. Take care here. As you round the corner, Worsbrough church is on the left and the Edmunds Arms on the right. Both are worth a visit. The church has Norman foundations but is mainly 13th century. Like many churches, it is dedicated to St Mary. There is a fine east window and some impressive carved timberwork, including an effigy of Sir Roger Rockley.

Using the Edmunds Arms pub purely as a landmark, go left and then left again into Priory Close. Almost at once there is a sign on the left pointing up the driveway of a house, indicating a footpath to Worsbrough Mill and Rockley Old Hall. This is your route. Before you end up in the garage, go through a gap on the right, into the field.

A test in navigation and patience

At this point all semblance of a path vanishes. Close study of the 1:25000 map seems to indicate that one path goes sharp right just inside the field and indeed there is a track here, heading past the sheds. The map also indicates that the path you want (to Rockley Old Hall), bears right to pass between the first and second sheds. There are no signs of this path on the ground.

On the reconnaissance, we tried various routes. The nearest approach to the line shown on the map is as follows; Turn sharp right on entering the field and pass to the right of the first shed. Just beyond the shed, turn left and go along the track until you are midway between the first and second shed. Here bear right and leave the track, making your way through pathless, waist high rough grass, thistles and willow herb, to a stile in the fence at the corner of the wood. This is a well-hidden stile, nearly covered in willow herb and elder. It lies to the right of a solitary oak.

There is some evidence that locals do not bother with the route described, but go straight on in the first field, keeping the sheds to the right. In this manner they reach a fence. There is evidence that people have climbed the fence and made their way across the next field to a stile in the bottom left-hand corner. Of course, no self respecting user of this book would do such a thing.

Having found the true path and the stile by the oak, negotiate the structure and follow the fence on the right alongside the wood. In this manner you will reach a further stile, of decidedly rickety construction, which leads into the wood. (This is the stile mentioned in the previous paragraph). Once inside the wood there are paths in all directions, most of which seem to be of dubious validity. The right of way lies straight ahead, down the steps to a stile into a field.

As you emerge from the trees you can see Emley Moor TV mast. Go straight across the field to a stile in the wall, marked by a signpost. (A curious feature of this walk was the number of traffic cones which seemed to crop up in the most unlikely places. For instance there was one in the middle of this field). The stile deposits you onto the main A61 road.

Rockley Old Hall – almost

Cross the A61 to a stile, signed to Rockley Old Hall. This can be seen ahead, a fine 16th/17th century building, its setting somewhat marred by the proximity of the M1. Go over the stile into the field and descend the path, which soon bears left along a terrace. The path passes through an area of scrubby hawthorn. Ignore the narrower path leading off to the right and continue down, through the scrub to a stile by a tall post.

Back into the Country Park

Beyond this point the overgrown reservoir comes into view on the right. Stepping stones lead across a boggy patch to a stile which takes you back into the country park. There had been a very dry spell just before this walk was tested, but it is likely that in normal conditions, this stretch could be very muddy. Once inside the country park, do not follow the path to the left, over the bridge, but go right instead, keeping the stream to your left. Soon another bridge is reached and here you do go left and cross the Rockley Dike. Follow the path round to the right, with a ditch on the left and the marsh on the right. You are now well and truly in the country park, with an ample provision of seats and a well-defined, well-maintained path.

Soon a cross "roads" of paths is reached. Go straight on here. Now, on the right there are glimpses of open water. Soon a path on the right leads to a wooden bird hide. Even if you are not a keen bird watcher, it is worth deviating into the hide to watch the antics of the numerous different types of bird. There's usually someone in the hide to explain what's in view, but please keep quiet. A pair of binoculars will certainly come in handy at this point.

On leaving the hide go right, still on the path round the perimeter of the lake. The wall of the dam can be seen to the right as can the tops of the mill buildings. A path diverges to the left over a bridge but ignore this and carry on, taking care to keep out of the way of errant mountain bikers. The perimeter path soon reaches a bridge across the inlet stream, the infant Dove, though known at this point as the Brough Green Brook. Soon you reach a junction of paths. The route ahead leads up onto the Dove Valley Trail which is visited by another of these walks, but your route lies to the right. This end of the reservoir is heavily overgrown, but the path soon comes alongside open water again and continues by the lakeside.

At the dam, go right and walk across the reservoir wall, noting on the left the old and new bridges over the spillway and river. At the end of the dam, bear left alongside the millpond and millrace, thus making your way back to the mill shop and museum. Time now for a cup of tea, an ice cream, a visit to the restored water mill and a leisurely look at the museum and information centre before going back to your car or to the bus stop.

Afterword . . . and thanks

I'd like to offer a word of thanks to all those friends who have accompanied me on these various walks. Sceptical they may have been at the start, but even those who ventured through Kiveton Colliery yard agreed that it was "a different experience". Particular thanks to my wife, who not only had to enjoy the walks, but also has had to put up with the hours of word processing, map drawing and proof checking, that go into books like this. Any mistakes in the book are mine, so I expect to be cursed more than once.

I would like to dedicate this book to my father, who sadly died whilst I was in the process of researching the walks. I owe to him my love of walking and it gave him great pleasure to see his enthusiasm for rambling translated into these books. Thanks Dad!

Martin Smith